UITGAVEN VAN HET
NEDERLANDS HISTORISCH-ARCHAEOLOGISCH INSTITUUT TE İSTANBUL

Publications de l' Institut historique et archéologique néerlandais de Stamboul

onder redactie van
A. A. CENSE en A. A. KAMPMAN

II

THE *NEZER* AND THE SUBMISSION IN SUFFERING HYMN FROM THE DEAD SEA SCROLLS

THE *NEZER* AND THE SUBMISSION IN SUFFERING HYMN FROM THE DEAD SEA SCROLLS

Reconstructed, Vocalized and Translated
with Critical Notes

BY

MEIR WALLENSTEIN, M.A., Ph. D.

Senior Lecturer in Medieval and Modern Hebrew at the University of Manchester

İSTANBUL
NEDERLANDS HISTORISCH-ARCHAEOLOGISCH INSTITUUT
IN HET NABIJE OOSTEN
1957

CONTENTS

Facsimiles (loose).

ABBREVIATIONS

Bar = Baruch

BASOR = Bulletin of the American Schools of Oriental Research, New Haven

BDB = Hebrew and English Lexicon of the O.T., by F. Brown etc.

BI = Thesaurus Totius Hebraitatis, E. Ben-Iehuda

CNSI = A Text-Book of North-Semitic Inscriptions, by A. Cooke, Oxford, 1903

DBS = The Book of Samuel, by S. R. Driver, Oxford, 1913

DHT = A Treatise on the Use of the Tenses in Hebrew, by S. R. Driver, Oxford, 1892

EMNM = *Mabho' le-Nosaḥ ha--Mishnah,* by J. N. Epstein, Jerusalem, 1948

En. = Enoch

IEJ = Israel Exploration Journal, Jerusalem

JSS = Journal of Semitic Studies, Manchester

KK = Biblia Hebraica, ed. R. Kittel and P. Kahle

O = *'Oẓar ha-Megilloth ha-Genuzoth,* ed. E. L. Sukenik, Jerusalem, 1955

Ps. Sol. = Psalms of Solomon

1Q = Qumran Cave I, by D. Barthelemy, and J. T. Milik etc., Oxford, 1955

1QH = The Hymns in *'Oẓar ha-Megilloth etc.*

1QIa = The Isaiah Scroll in The Dead Sea Scrolls of St. Mark's Monastery, vol. I, ed. Millar Burrows, etc., New-Haven, 1950

1QIb = Isaiah in *'Oẓar ha-Megilloth etc.*

1QPHa = The Habakkuk Commentary in The Dead Sea Scrolls etc., ed. Burrows

1QS = Manual of Discipline in The Dead Sea Scrolls etc., vol. II, ed. Burrows, 1951

1QW = The War of the Children of Light etc. in *'Oẓar ha-Megilloth etc.*

Jub. = Jubilees

QSS = *Sepher ha-Shorashim la-RaDaQ,* Venice, 1529

R = Restoration of lacunae in the MS

RZD = The Zadokite Documents, ed. C. Rabin, Oxford, 1954

Test. Ben. = Testament of Benjamin

Test. Jud. = Testament of Judah

VT = Vetus Testamentum, Leiden

WHR = A Striking Hymn etc., by M. Wallenstein in Bulletin of the John Rylands Library, vol. 38, no. 1, September, 1955

YKS = The Dead Sea Scrolls etc., by H. Yalon in *Kirjath Sepher,* vol. xxvii, no. 2-3

YM = The Scroll of the War of the Sons of Light etc., by Y. Yadin, Jerusalem, 1955

ZPY = *Piyyuṭe Yannai,* by M. Zulay, Jerusalem, 1938

INTRODUCTION

The following hymn, drawn from the 'Oẓar plates XLII and XLIII, is one of the more peculiar linguistically and syntactically, and the longest, amongst the thirty or so hymns and parts of hymns included in the 'Oẓar. It is also one of the more important hymns as far as its subject matter is concerned. In it are expressed, besides various other data as well as tenets of the Sect thrown out here and there in a fragmentary manner, two well-developed ideas of paramount importance. The first idea is the more fully developed. In line 6 is set forth the notion of the choice and "everlasting branch", hidden at a "secret fount", in a concise form, after which is spun a long and *continuous* elaboration of the theme. The second idea, which is also conspicuously developed but less sequentially set forth, before which comes a lyrical effusion which speaks about sufferings in detail, is that of the joy in tribulation.

In the final assessment of the diversified phenomena of the Scrolls in general and the Hymns in particular the present hymn is bound to play a significant role, and it is hoped that the attempted translation along with the elaborate apparatus which includes a full vocalization according to the Ben-Asher system of our printed Hebrew Bibles will be of some help in this respect. Here is the place to say that one fully realizes the incongruity of clothing this ancient text with a Masoretic apparel. Indeed, with regard to the pointing of some of its forms one feels somewhat guilty of being procrustean, using as it were violent methods in order to reduce them to uniformity. However, the expository element amply inherent in this vocalization should perhaps justify its inclusion in this difficult text.

The author wishes to record his indebtedness to Mosad Bialik, Jerusalem, Israel, for kindly allowing him to reproduce here the relevant facsimiles from 'Oẓar and to Prof. J. van der Ploeg who has recommended this work for publication in the series «Uitgaven van het Nederlands Historisch-Archaeologisch Instituut te Istanbul».

Manchester, September 1957   M. WALLENSTEIN

Plate XLII

From *'Oẓar ha-Megilloth ha-Genuzoth*, ed. E. L. Sukenik (1955)

Plate XLIII

From ʾOẓar ha-Megilloth ha-Genuzoth, ed. E. L. Sukenik (1955)

PL. XLII

אֹו]דְכָה אֲדֹו נָי   4

כִּי נְ]תַתַּנִי[2] בִּמְקֹור[3] נֹו זְלִים[4] בַּיַבָּשָׁה[4]

וּמַבּוּעַ מַיִם בְּאֶרֶץ צִיָּה[5]

וּמַ]שְׁקֵי גַן[6] [בַּעֲרָבָה[7]   5

נָאֶ]הְ[יֶ]ה[8] מַטַּע[9] בְּרֹושׁ וְתִדְהָר עִם תְּאַשּׁוּר יַחַד לִכְבֹו דְכָה[10]   5

❋   ❋

❋

עֲצֵי חַיִּים[11] בְּמַעְיָן[12] רָז[13] מְחוּבָּאִים[14] בְּתֹוךְ כָּל־עֲצֵי מַיִם[15]   6

יִהְיוּ[16] לְהַפְרִיחַ[17] נֵצֶר[18] לְמַטַּעַת[19] עֹולָם[20]

לְהַשְׁרִישׁ[21] טֶרֶם יַפְרִיחוּ[22]   7

וְשׁוּרָשֵׁיהֶם[23] לְיוּבָל[ ]יְשַׁלֵּחוּ[25]

וַיִּפְתַּח[26] לְמַיִם חַיִּים[27]

וַיְגִזְעוּ וַיְהִי[28] לְמְקֹור עֹולָם[29]   10   8

וּבִנְצֶר עָלֵיהוּ[30] יִרְעוּ כָּל־[חַיֹּות[31]]יָעַר

וּמִרְמָס גִּזְעֹו[32] לְכָל־עֹו בְרֵי[33] דָרֶךְ   9

וְדָלִיֹּתֹו לְכָל־עֹוף כָּנָף[34]

וַיִּרְמּו[35] עָלֵיהוּ כָּל־עֲ[צֵי[36]]מָיִם

כִּי בְּמַטָּעָתָם[37] יִתְשַׂגְשָׂגוּ[38]   15

וְאֶל[39] יוּבַל לֹא יְשַׁלֵּחוּ[40] שֹׁורֶשׁ   10

וּמַפְרִיחַ[41] נֵצֶר קֹ[נ]וֹ[42] [דֶשֶׁ]א[ ]לְמַטַּעַת אֱמֶת ﬞ ﬞ סוּתָּר[44]

בְּלוֹא[45] נֶחְשָׁב[46]   11

וּבְלֹא[47] נוֹדַע חוֹתָם רָזוֹ[48]

וְ ﬞ בָּ ﬞ תָּ[נ]ה א[ ]ל[49]   20

שַׂכְתָּה[50] בְּעַד פִּרְיוֹ בְּרָז גִּבּוֹרֵי כֹחַ[51]

וְרוּחוֹת קֹדֶשׁ[52]   12

וְלַהַט אֵשׁ מִתְהַפֶּכֶת[53]

פַּל יָ[נֵ]רֹוֹ[54] מִפְּנֵי[55] [ ]מַעַיַּן[56] חַיִּים[57]

וְעִם עֲצֵי עוֹלָם[58] לֹא יִשְׁתֶּה מֵי קוֹדֶשׁ[59]   25   13

פַּל יְנוֹבֵב פִּרְיוֹ עִם[ ]מַ[זֵר]עַ[60] שְׁחָקִים[61]

כִּי רָאָה בְּלֹא[62] הִכִּיר[63]

וַיַּחְשֹׁב בְּלֹא הֶאֱמִין לִמְקוֹר[64] חַיִּים[65]   14

וַיִּתֵּן[66] יָ[פֶ]ר[67] [חַ]ל[ ]עוֹלָם[68]

וַאֲנִי הָיִיתִי לְ[נ]בַ[69] נְהָרֹת[70] שׁוֹטְפִים[71]   30   15

כִּי[72] גָרְשׁוּ ﬞ עָלַי רִפְשָׁם[73]

*   *

*

וְאַתָּה אֵל[ ]לָ[74]   16

שַׂמְתָּה בְּפִ[75] כְּיוֹרֶה גֶּשֶׁם לְכוֹל-[דֹּו]רְשׁוֹ[76]

וּמַבּוּעַ מַיִם חַיִּים וְלֹא יְכַזֵּב

לִפְתוֹחַ[77] הַשָּׁ[ ]ק[מִ]ים[78] וְלֹא[80] יָמִישׁוּ[82]   35   17

וְיִהְיֶה לְנַחַל שׁוֹטֵף[83] עַ]ד אֵין גְּבוּל[מָיִם

וּלְיַמִּים לְאֵין חֵקֶ]ר[85]

פִּתְאֹם[86] יַבִּיעוּ[87] מְחֻבָּאִים בַּסֵּתֶר[88]]   18

וְיִהְיוּ[89] לְמַיִן[יָם[90] גּוֹרְפִים[91]]לָח וְיָבֵשׁ[92]   19

מְצוּלָה[93] לְכֹל-חַיָּה וָעָ]וֹף   40

וְיַצְלִילוּם[94] כַּ]עוֹפֶרֶת בְּמַיִם אַדִּירִי]ם[95]

וְיַעֲלוּ בָּאֵשׁ[96] וַיְבַשֵּׁן[97]   20

וּמַטַּע פְּרִי[98]]מַעְיַן רָז יְהִי לְנֶ]צֶר[99] עוֹלָם

לְעֵדֶן כָּבוֹד וּפֶ[100]]תְּהִלָּה[101]

וּבְיָדִי פְּתַחְתָּה מְקוֹרָם[102] עִם מְפֻלְגִין[103]   45 21   ם]

לִפְנוֹת[104] עַל[105] קַו נָכוֹן

וּמַטַּע עֵצֵיהֶם[106] עַל מִשְׁקֹלֶת הַשֶּׁמֶשׁ[107]   22

לֹא]יִיבַשׁ[108][

וְהָיָה כַּ]גַּן[109] לְפַאֲרֶת[110] כָּבוֹד

בְּהַנִיפִי יָד[111] לְעֻזּוּק[112] פְּלַגָּיו[113]   50 23

יַפוּ שָׁרָשָׁיו בְּצוּר חַלָּמִישׁ[114]

וְ]יוֹנְקֵי[יִשְׁרֹ[115]ג[בְּאֶרֶץ גִּזְעָם

וּבְעֵת חֹם יַעֲצֹר מָעֹז[116]   24

וְאִם אָשִׁיב יָד[117]

יִהְיֶה כְּעַרְעָ]ר[118] בָּעֲרָבָה[119]   55

גֻּזְעוֹ כַּחֲרֵלִים בַּמְּלֵחָה[120]

וּפְלַגָּיו[122] יַעַל קוֹץ[123] וְדַרְדַּר[124]   25

לְשָׁמִיר וָשַׁיִת יִ[ן]הְיֶה[124]

וְעֵצֵי[ ] שְׂפָתוֹ[124] יֵהָפְכוּ כַּעֲצֵי בְאוּשִׁים[127]

לִפְנֵי חֹם יִבּוֹל עָלָיו[127]   60   26

וְלֹא נִפְתַּח עִם מְכוֹר [מָיִם[129]

*   *   *

*

מִסָּבִיב[ ][130] מָגוֹר עִם חֻלָיִים

וּמִ[נֶּגֶב[131] עַל[לְבָנ]ִי[132] [בִּ]נְגוֹעִים[133]   27

וָאֶהְיֶה כְאִישׁ נֶעֱזָב בְּ[134]   [

וְאֵין[ ]מָעוֹז לּוֹ[136]   65

כִּי פָרַח נִגְ[עוֹ][137] עָלַי[ ]לְמַרוֹרִים[138]   28

וּכְאוֹב אָנוּשׁ לְאֵין עֲצוֹר[139]

[וְ]נַפְשִׁי הִשְׁתּוֹמֵ[מָה][141] עָלַי כְּיוֹרְדֵי שְׁאוֹל

וְעִם מֵתִים יְחַפֵּשׂ רוּחִי[142]   29

כִּי הִגִּיעוּ לְשַׁחַת חַ[יָּ]י[143]   70

וְעָלַי[ ]תִּתְעַטֵּף נַפְשִׁי יוֹמָם וְלַיְלָה לְאֵין מָנוֹחַ[145]   30

וַיִּפְרַח כָּאֵשׁ בֹּעֵר עָצוּר בְּ[עַצְמוֹתָי[147]

עַ[ד]יָמִּימָה[148] תּוֹאכַל[149] שַׁלְהַבְתָּהּ[150]

לְהָתֵם כֹּחַ לִקְצָיִם   31

וּלְכַלּוֹת בָּשָׂר עַד מוֹעֲדִים[151]   75

וַיִּתְעוֹפְפֶן ֭וּ] חֲצֵי מִשְׁבָּרִים [153] [152]

32 וְנַפְשִׁי עָלַי תִּשְׁתּוֹחַח לְכַלֵּה [154]

כִּי נִשְׁבַּת מָעוּזִי מִגְּוִיָּתִי [155]

וַיִּנָּגֶר כַּמַּיִם לִבִּי [156]

33 80 וַיִּמַּס כַּדּוֹנַג בְּשָׂרִי [157]

וּמָעוֹז מָתְנַי הָיָה לְבֶהָלָה [158]

וַתִּשָּׁבֵר זְרוֹעִי מִקָּנֶהָ [159]

[וָאֵי]ן לְהָנִיף יָד [160]

34 [וָרַג]לִי בְּלִכְדָהּ בַּכֶּבֶל [161] [162] [163]

85 וַיֵּלְכוּ כַמַּיִם בִּרְכַּי [164]

וְאֵין לִשְׁלוֹחַ פָּעַם [165]

וְלֹא מִצְעַד לְקוֹל רַגְלִי [166] [167]

35 וְכֹל-מִצְעֲדֵי רוֹתְּקוּ בְּזִקֵּי מִכְשׁוֹל [168] [170]

וּלְשׁוֹן הַגְּבַרְתָּה פִּפִּי בְּלֹא [171] [172] [173]

90 נֶאֱסָפָה [174]

36 וְאֵין לְהָרִים קוֹל [175]

[וְאֵין לְשׁ]וֹ[ן] לְמֻדִּים לְהַחֲיוֹת רוּחַ כּוֹשְׁלִים [176] [177] [178]

וְלָעוּת לְעָאֵף דָּבָר [179] [180]

37 נֶאֱלַם קוֹל שְׂפָתַי מִפִּי [181]

95 וַיֵּ[אָסֵר] בְּזִקֵּי מִשְׁפָּט [182] [183] [184]

לִבִּי לִבִּי פּוֹתְנָה [185] [186] [187]

קִירוֹ[תָיו[188]]מָל[אוּ בַּמְרוֹרִי]ם[189]

וְאֵין לְהָבִין[170]]לְבַב נִמְהָרִים[171] מְמֻשָׁל[192]

מָל[38

שׁ[הַתֵּבֵל[   ]לִים וַא[100

נֶאֶלְמוּ פָּ]אֵין[39

אֱנוֹשׁ לאָ]נ[40

         PL. XLIII

אפ]ן[193]   1

עֵ]י]נַי[194] ל[א] תָנוּם בַּלַּיְלָה[196]   2

]נ[197]   לְאֵ]ין[198] רַחֲמִים   105   3

בְּאַף יְעוֹרֵר קִנְאָה[199]

וּלְכַלֵּה[200]

]וַאֲנִי אֲפַפוּנִי[201]]מִשְׁבְּרֵי מָוֶת

וּשְׁאוֹל עַל יְצוּעַי עַרְשׂוּ[202]

בְּקִינָה תִּשָּׂא מְ]נ[שָׁתִי[203]   110

בְּקוֹל[204] אֲנָחָה[205]

עֵינַי כְּעָשׁ[206] בְּכִבְשָׁן   5

וְדִמְעָתִי כְּנַחֲלֵי מָיִם[207]

כָּלוּ לְמָנוֹחַ עֵינַי[208]

]רֵעַי[209]]יַ[210] עַמֹד[210] מֵרָחוֹק   115   6

וְחִוַּי מִצַּד[211]

וַאֲנִי מִשָּׂאָה אֶלְמֹשׁוֹאָה[212]

וּמִמַּכְאוֹב לְנֶגַע[213]

וּמְחַבְּלִים לְמִשְׁבָּרִים[214]   7

תִּשְׁתּוֹחַח נַפְשִׁי בְּנִפְלְאוֹתֶיכָה[215]   120

וְלֹא הִזְנַחְתַּנִי בְּחַסְדֵּיכָה[216]

[מ]קֵץ לְקֵץ תִּשְׁתַּשַׁע נַפְשִׁי בַּהֲמוֹן רַחֲמֶיכָה[217] [218]   8

וְאָשִׁיבָה לִמְבַלְעֵי דָבָר[219]

וְלִמְשַׁתּוֹחֲחִי בִי תּוֹכַחַת[220] [221]   9

וְאַרְשִׁיעָה דִּינוֹ   125

וּמִשְׁפָּטְכָה אַצְדִּיק[222]

כִּי יָדַעְתִּי בַאֲמִתֶּכָה[223]   10

וָאֶבְחֲרָה בְּמִשְׁפָּטִי[224]

וּבְנִגּוּעַי רָצִיתִי[225] [226]

כִּי יִחַלְתִּי לְחַסְדֵּיכָה[227]   130

נַתַן תְּחִנָּה בְּפִי עַבְדֶּכָה[228] [229]   11

וְלֹא גָעַרְתָּה חַיָּי[230]

וּשְׁלוֹמִי לֹא הִזְנַחְתָּה[231]

וְלֹא עָזַבְתָּה תִּקְוָתִי[232] [233]   12

וְלִפְנֵי נֶגַע הֶעֱמַדְתָּה רוּחִי[234]   135

כִּי אַתָּה יְסַדְתָּה רוּחִי[235]

וַתֵּדַע מְזִמָּתִי[236] [237]

וּבְצוּקוֹתַי נִחַמְתַּנִי[238]   13

וּבִסְלִיחֹנֹת אֶשְׁתַּעֲשַׁע[240] [239]

140 וָאֶנָּחֲמָה עַל פֶּשַׁע רִאשׁוֹן[241]

14 וָאֵדְעָה כִּי יֵשׁ מִקְוָה בַּ[חַ]סָדֶיכָה[243] [242]

וְתוֹחֶלֶת[244] בְּרוֹ ב-כּוֹחֲכָה[245]

15 כִּי לֹא יִצְדַּק כּוֹל בְּמִ[שְׁפָּ]טֶכָה[246]

וְלֹא יִזְ[כֶּ]ה בְּ[רִי]רִיבְכָה[247]

145 אֱנוֹשׁ מֵאֱנוֹשׁ יִצְדָּק

16 וְגֶבֶר [מִגֶּבֶ]ר יַשְׂכִּיל[248]

וּבָשָׂר מִיֵּצֶר [בָּשָׂר] יִכְבַּד[249]

וְרוּחַ מֵרוּחַ תִּגְבַּר[250]

17 וְכִגְבֻ[רַ]תְ[כָה]כָה אֵין בְּכוֹחַ[252] [251]

150 וְלִכְבוֹדְכָה אֵין [קֵץ[253]

וּ]לְחָכְמָתְכָה אֵין מִדָּה[254]

וְלֶאֱמֻ[נָ]תְכָה אֵין [קֵצֶ]ה[256] [255]

18 וּלְכוֹל-הַנֶּעֱזָב מִמֶּנָּה [257]

וַאֲנִי בְּכָה הַצַּ[לְ]תִּי נַפְשִׁי[258]

155 19 כִּי אַתָּה[259] עִמָּדִי

וְלֹא הֵסַ[נ]יְרוֹתָה חַסְדְּכָה מִנַּפְ[שִׁי[261] [260]

20 [ ] וּכְזוֹמֵם לִי תָ[גָ]עָשֶׂה לְצָרִי[264] [262] [263]

אִם לִכְלִמָּ]ה וְאִם לְבוֹשֶׁת פָּנִים[266] [265]

21 כִּי [ ] לִי

160 וְאַתָּה בְּרֹ[וב-חַסְדֶּכָה אַל] תַּגְבֵּר צָרַי עָלַי לְמִכְשֹׁול לִי [268] [267]

22 [וְהָבֵא לְכֹו]לֹ-אַנְשֵׁי מִלְחַמ[תִּי וְיָרִיבַי בֹּו]שֶׁת פָּנִים [269]

וּכְלִמָּה לְנַרְגְּנַי בִּי [270]

23 כִּי אַתָּה אֵלִי לְמֵעֹ[וֹם הַגַּלְדִּי [272] [271]

וְאַתָּה] תָּרִיב רִיבִי [273]

165 כִּי בְּרָז חָכְמָתְכָה הֹוכַחְתָּה בִּי [275] [274]

24 וַתַּחְבֵּא אֱמֶת לְקֵ[ץ]צָה [276]

וְשָׁלֹום לְ]מֹועֲדֹו [277]

וַתְּהִי תֹוֹכַחְתְּכָה לִי לְשִׂמְחָה וּלְשָׂשֹׂו[ן [278]

25 וּנְגֹועַי לְמַרְפֵּא עֹו[לָם וְלַאֲרוֹכַת]נֶצַח [280] [279]

170 וּבֹוז צָרַי לִי לִכְלִיל כָּבֹוד [282] [281]

26 וְכִשְׁלֹוֹנִי לִגְבוּרַת עֹולָם [283]

כִּי בְשִׂ[ן]כִלְכָה הִשְׂכַּלְתִּי [284]

וּבִכְבֹוֹדְכָה הֹופִיעַ אֹורִי [285]

27 כִּי מָאֹור מֵחֹושֶׁךְ הַאִירֹותָה לִי [286]

175 [וַתִּתֵּן מַרְפֵּא לְמַח]ץ מַכְתִי [287]

וּלְמִכְשֹׁולִי לִי גְּבוּרַת פֶּלֶא [288]

28 וּרְחֹו[ב]עֹולָם בְּצָרַת נַפֶ[ן]שִׁי [290] [289]

אַתָּה] מְנֹוסִי [291]

מִשְׂגַּבִּי

180 סֶלַע עֻו[זִּי]וּמְצֹו[דָתִי [292]

בְּכָה אֶחְסָיָה[293]   29

מִכּוּל-מְכַ[שׁוֹל תִּהְיֶה][294] לִי לְפַלֵּט עַד עוֹלָם[295]

כִּי אַתָּה מֵאָבִי[296] יְדַעְתָּנִי[297]   30

וּמֵרֶחֶם [סְמַכְתָּנִי]

וּמִבֶּטֶן[298] אִמִּי גְּמַלְתָּה עָלַי[299]   185

וּמִשַּׁדֵּי הוֹרָתִי[300] רַחֲמֶיךָ לִי[301]   31

וּבְחֵיק אוֹמַנְתִּי [תְּשַׁעַשְׁעֵנִי][302]

וּמִנְּעוּרַי הוֹפַעְתָּה לִי בְּשֵׂכֶל מִשְׁפָּטֶכָה[303]

וּבֶאֱמֶת נָכוֹן סְמַכְתָּנִי[304]   32

וּבְרוּחַ קָוּדְשֶׁכָה תְּשַׁעַשְׁעֵנִי[305]   190

וְעַד הַיּוֹם [בַּחַנְתָּ]ה[306] לְ[נ]בִּ[י][307]

וְתוֹכַחַת צִדְקָכָה עִם נַ[עַ]וּתִי[308]   33

וּמִשְׁמַר שְׁלוֹמְכָה[309] לְפַלֵּט[310] נַפְשִׁי[311][312]

וְעִם מִצְעָדִי[313] רוֹב-סְלִיחוֹת[314][315]   34

וַהֲמוֹן [רַח]מִים[316] בְּהַשְׁפָּטְכָה בִּי[317]   195

וְעַד שֵׂיבָה אַתָּה תְּכַלְכְּלֵנִי[318]

כִּי אָבִי לֹא יְדָעַנִי   35

וְאִמִּי עָלֶיךָ עֲזָבָתַנִי[319]

כִּי אַתָּה אָב לְכוּל-[בְּנֵ][320]י אֲמִתְּכָה[321]

וְתָגֵל עֲלֵיהֶם כִּמְרַחֶמֶת[322] עַל עוּלָהּ[323]   200   36

וּכְאוֹמֵן בְּחֵיק תְּכַלְכֵּל לְכוּל-מַעֲשֶׂ[י][כָה][324]

TRANSLATION

I [thank thee, O Lord,

For] thou hast set me at a streaming fountain in dry ground,

And (at) a well of water in parched land,

And (at) garden-irrigating water [in the desert.

5 I thus tu]rned, for the sake of thy glory, into a plantation of the fir tree
    and the pine and the box-tree together.

* *
*

Trees of life at a secret fount, hidden amongst all the trees by the water,
    are about to blossom forth a branch to become an everlasting plant.

It will strike roots ere they will blossom forth,

And ere they will spread out their roots by the river.

And it will open to (absorb) living water,

10 Its stem becoming an everlasting stem.

And at the covering of its leaves shall graze all the [beasts of] the forest.

And its trunk shall be a treading-place for all that pass by,

And (so will) its bough (be) for all winged fowl.

But all the tr[ees by the] water will outgrow it in height,

15 For they will flourish at their plantation,

Though not spreading root towards the river.

Thus that which has blossomed forth as a holy branch to become a
    truthful bough will be concealed,

Neither to be accounted,

Nor the seal of its secret to be known.

20 Moreover, thou, [O Go]d,

Hast hedged about its fruit with the secret of the mighty in strength,

And the holy spirits,

And the glow of revolving fire,

So that one shall neither have [his fill] of the well-[water of] (the
    trees) of life,

25 Nor drink the water of the holy (branch) together with the everlasting
    trees,

Nor make its fruit flourish with [the see]d of heaven.

Indeed, one (who may) see (it) will not identify (it),

And one (who may) reflect (upon it) will not believe (it) to be a branch
   of life,
Capable of producing an everlasting [blo]ssom.
30 I thus became the [des]pised amongst the overflowing rivers,
For indeed they have cast upon me their mire.

*   *
*

And thou, my God,
Hast put in my mouth rain (which is as welcome) to all [that seek it]
   as is the first rain,
And a spring of living water that will not fail.
35 The fountains will open, not ceasing,
Thus turning into a river [exeedingly] overflowing with water;
Yea, into immeasurable seas.
Suddenly will (also) the well-hidden (waters) [   ] issue forth,
And turn into water[s sweeping away] (every) green and dry (tree) —
40 (Even the) cover for all the beasts and f[owls,
Sinking them like] lead in mighty waters.
And (in the course of time) they will emit an ill odour and dry up.
But the fruit branch of [the secret fount will turn into] an everlasting
   [bra]nch;
Yea, into a glorious delight and a [praiseworthy] crown.
45 Truly, it was by my hand that thou hast opened their source beside the
      channels of [   ],
In order to turn (them) towards the right direction,
And the plantation of their trees towards the "sun-level",
So that it [wither] not,
[And its sto]ck [turns] into a glorious bough.
50 When I reach out (my) hand to dig about its bed,
Its roots strike (even) into rocky flint,
And the stocks of [its saplings take root] in the earth.
It retains its strength even at the hot season.
But if I turn back my hand,
55 It becomes as a solitary bu[sh in the wilderness],
Its stem as nettles in the salt-plain,
And its bed yields thorns and thistles,
Becoming briers and wild growth,
[And the trees] (growing at) its border become like worthless trees,
60 Its foliage languishes before the heat,
For it does not open (though it be) beside the source of [water].

*   *
*

Terror and diseases [are round about] (me),

And [my] heart is [stri]cken with plagues.

Yea, I am as a forsaken man in [   ],

65 Having no vigour,

For my wound has broken forth and become sore,

And (is causing me) desperate pain without restraint,

[And my heart is desola]te within me like that of those who go down
  into Sheol,

And my spirit is adrift amongst the dead.

70 Verily, [my] li[fe] draws nigh unto the grave,

[And] my soul faints (within me) day and night without rest.

And it broke forth like fire shut up in [my bones],

Its flame consuming ev[en] to the depths,

Thus destroying the strength before the Time is due,

75 And exhausting the flesh ere the approach of the Season.

And destroying arrows fly about,

And my soul is utterly depressed,

For my strength has been drained from my body.

And my heart is running out like water,

80 And my flesh melts away like wax,

And the vigour of my loins turns into nought,

My arm was broken from (its) bone,

[Thus I canno]t lift up my hand,

And my foot is caught in fetters,

85 And my knees are as weak as water,

Thus I cannot take a pace,

And my foot-fall emits no sound.

Indeed, all my steps are bound with fetters that trip me up.

And as to (my) tongue that thou hast made strong in my mouth, it is
  worn out,

90 It has ceased to function.

Thus I cannot lift up my voice,

[And there is neither a ton]gue of the learned to revive the spirit of
  the stumblers,

Nor a word with which to enlighten the weary,

The sound of my speech is dumb in my mouth,

95 For it [is bound] with restricting fetters.

My heart, my heart is enti[ced],

Its [wall]s are fi[lled] with bitterness,

[And I cannot make] the heart of the eager [understand] wisdom.

               ] ~ [

100   ] ~ ~ ~ ~ [   ]- the world [
                  ] they turn dumb as things non-existent.
                  ] a man ~-[
          ]~-[
          ] [my ey]e does n[ot] slumber at night,
105 [   ] without mercy.
He stirs up jealousy angrily,
With intent to destroy.
[And I am encompassed] by waves of death.
Hell is my couch.
110 [My be]d raises a lament,
Yea, a groaning sound.
My eyes are (consumed) like a moth in a kiln,
And my tears are like rivers of water.
(Indeed), my eyes fail for rest.
115 [My friend] stands far off,
 And my kinsman is aloof.
But (though) I am (driven) from devastation to desolation,
From pain to affliction,
And from pangs to calamities,
120 My soul ever meditates on thy wonderful works,
Since in thy kindness thou hast not forsaken me.
My soul takes delight [from] season to season in the multitude of thy
    mercies,
And I have a word with which to answer him that swallows me,
And an argument against him that slanders me.
125 I shall surely pronounce him guilty,
And declare thy judgement just,
For I know thy truth.
Yea, I choose my punishment,
And wish my suffering,
130 For I am waiting for thy kindness.
Thou hast indeed given supplication into the mouth of thy servant,
Not withdrawing my maintenance,
And not forsaking my welfare,
 And not shaking my hope,
135 But fortifying my spirit to face suffering.
Verily, thou hast established my spirit,
And thou knowest my devisings,
And thou hast comforted me in my distress,
And I delight in (thy) forgiveness.

140 I regret the Original Sin,
But I know that there is hope through thy [kin]dness,
And expectancy through the multitude of thy strength.
Verily, none would be justified in a jud[gemen]t with thee,
Nor would he be clean in a dispute with thee.

145 (For only) a human being can (prove) more righteous than (his) neighbour;
And a man more skilful [than (his) fel]low;
And (a creature framed of) flesh more distinguished than (his) [flesh-] created friend;
And spirit stronger than spirit.
But there is nothing like thy streng[th] in the (domain) of power.

150 And there is no [limit] to thy honour,
Nor a measure to thy wisdom,
[Nor] a bou[ndary] to thy tru[th].
Yea, he who neglects it [   ].
But as for me, [I] have sav[ed my soul] through thee,

155 [For thou art] with me.
Thou didst not re[move thy kindness from] my [so]ul.
[   ] and thou wilt [do unto my adversaries] as they thought
to have done to me,
[Whether ignomin]y or shame of face.
For [   ] to me.

160 And thou, with the multi[tude of thy kindness, do not] make my
adversaries prevail over me so as to make me stumble,
[Thus wilt thou bring upon a]ll [my] enemies [and my opponents
sha]me of face,
And upon those who backbite me, ignominy,
For thou art my God since the da[y of my birth,
And thou] wilt plead my cause.

165 Yea, it is with the secret of thy wisdom that thou hast chastened me,
Hiding truth until [its] (appropriate) Ti[me,
And peace until] its (allotted) Season.
Thus thy chastisement was unto me joy and rejoicing,
And my suffering an ev[erlasting] healing [and] an eternal [cure],

170 And the contempt of me by my adversaries, a crown of glory,
And my stumbling an ever-lasting strength.
Verily, through [thy] wis[dom I acquired understanding],
And through thy splendour my light shines,
For thou hast caused a luminary to shine out of darkness for me,

175 [And thou hast given healing to the sore]ness of my wound,

And a wonderful strength to my feebleness,
And utter deliverance in the adversity of [my so]ul.
[Thou art] my refuge,
My stronghold,
180 The rock of my strength and my fastness.
In thee do I seek protection.
For ever [hast thou been] my deliverance from every hard[ship].
Thou hast, indeed, disciplined me from my youth,
And [upheld me] from the womb.
185 [And] thou hast dealt bountifully with me [from] my mother's [belly],
And from the breasts of her that conceived me (thou hast shown) thy
    love towards me,
And while I was at the bosom of her that brought me up [thou hast
    fondled me],
And from my youth thou hast appeared unto me with thy wise instruction,
Sustaining me aright with truth,
190 And delighting me with thy holy spirit,
Even to this day thou [searchest] my hea[rt],
And thy righteous reproach is upon my transgression,
And thy secure guard is a refuge for my soul.
My steps are accompanied by an abundance of forgiveness,
195 And (I am granted) a multitude of mercy when thou executest
    judgement in me.
Thou wilt sustain me even when I am grey-headed,
For my father does not know me,
And my mother has abandoned me to thy charge.
Indeed, thou art surely a father to all thy children of truth,
200 Thau rejoicest over them as does a lovingmother over her suckling,
And sustainest all thy creature[s] as a foster-father (sustains a child)
    in his care.

———————

NOTES

1. This, O's R, is the most likely for it is the more common opening of the Hymns. For a different opening, see WHR, p. 242, n. 3.

2. For the meaning of נתן followed by *beth,* see Ez. xxxii, 23.

3. This participle pl. of נזל, "to flow", "to trickle", appears in the Bible (e.g., Ps. lxxviii, 16; Prov. v, 15), as it does also here, figuratively as parallel with *water.* In the post-Biblical literature it connotes any flowing liquid.

4. Cf. Is. xliv, 3.

5. Cf. Is. xxxv, 7; Ps. lxiii, 2; Ez. xix, 13; Note parallel with preceding line and cf. the following line.

6. Part of the *waw* and the whole of the *mem* of ומשקי are damaged. משקי = משקה, a common spelling in the Scrolls. See YM, p. 297b, n. on מראי (1. 12). To Yadin's examples one may perhaps add 1Q, p. 78, 1. 6; p. 154, 1. 7. In the light of the above it seems advisable to re-examine similar spellings in the Zadokite Document (e.g., RZD, p. 9, 1. 14). For Biblical examples, see Yalon, *Sinai* xxvi, p. 286. For a longer discussion of the interchange of final *yodh* and *he* in the Scrolls, see M. Gottstein, V.T., IV, 3, pp. 104-5. משקי גן, a metaphorical expression for water, is original. Cf., however, Cant. iv, 15. The translation "and a garden-irrigator", the hymnologist referring to himself as one who brings life to lifeless places, is also a possibility, although the parallel with its preceding lines would be somewhat impaired.

7. For R, cf. Is. xli, 19; li, 3. Other possible RR are במדבר (cf. Is. xliii, 20) and בישימון (cf. Is. xliii, 19; 20).

8. Part of the *yodh,* not recorded in O, seems to be visible.

9. Cf. 1QH, XLI, 19 (where ... מטע] ... is to be read instead of O's reading ... שע ~ ...). Its fem. counterpart appears further, lines 6; 15; 17 and also in 1QH, XL, 15. See n. 19.

10. In both Is. xli, 19 and lx, 13, whence the last few words are obviously drawn, the reading is ברוש תדהר ותאשור יחדו. Both 1QIa and 1QIb follow the M.T. here with some slight deviation. After לכבודכה there is a small space capable of containing about two letters. This may be due to either the copyist's desire to give some harmony to the position of words at

the end of the lines or more likely (as the copyist does not seem to have
taken too much pride in his copying) to the conclusion of the introductory
character of the hymn. The space here may also be due to a defect in
the parchment. Similar spaces are to be observed in 1QW. (See YM,
p. 249, and respective photographed illustrations which follow p. 244).

11. Cf. the sing. in Gen. ii, 9; iii, 22; 24, where the reference is to the tree
of the Garden of Eden and in Prov. iii, 18, where the reference is to the
Torah. In Ps. of Sol. xiv, 2, "trees of life" is used as an attribute for
God's pious ones "whose planting is rooted for ever". In II En. viii, 3
God is said to be resting at the tree of life whenever he comes to the
Garden of Eden.

12. For the force of the *beth* here, cf. במקור, line 2.

13. Perhaps a rendering of מעין חתום (Cant. iv, 12), רז being a very common
term in the Scrolls in general and in the Hymns in particular (see YM,
pp. 241-242). Targum's esoteric rendering of Cant. iv, 12 is of interest
here. In the Apocryphal literature terms denoting secret abound.

14. For the Pu'al, cf. Job xxiv, 4. For possible Pi'els in the Hymns, see
V.T., V, 3, p. 281, n. 6.

15. Cf. Ez. xxxi, 14. For superior trees growing *beyond* trees of less
importance, see I En. xxxii, 3.

16. First letter impaired. O reads והיו.

17. A transitive Hiph'il. Similarly, Ez. xvii, 24. For the peculiar usage of
היה followed by infinitive with *lamedh,* indicating destination, cf. Gen.
xv, 12; II Ch. xxvi, 5. See DHT, p. 275.

18. Cf. "And a branch shall grow out of his (Jesse's) roots" (Is. xi, 1).

19. Or לְמַטָּעַת, if the absolute is מַטָּעָה. מטעת, the fem. of מטע (see n. 9 above),
appears in the Talmudic literature in the construct state (e.g., Mid. Rab.
on Cant. ii, 3), having sometimes (cf. e.g., Tosephta Kil'ayim III, 3)
a slightly different connotation from that given to the Biblical מטע. In the
Zadokite Document (I, 7) we have מטעת (preceded by שורש) in the
absolute. (It is not clear why Charles (*Apocrypha . . . ,* II, p. 800, 5)
emends it to read מטעו on account of Is. lx, 21, in which שורש is not even
mentioned. See elaborate nn. 2 and 3 in RZD, I, 7).

20. Cf. 1QH, XL, 15; 1QS, VIII, 5; XI, 8. Cf. also I En. lxxxiv, 6.

21. Lit. "striking". The infinitive is used here gerundially. Similarly, Is.
xxi, 1; I Sam. xiv, 33. 1QW abounds in this and similar peculiar uses
of the infinitive. Cf. e.g. XVI, 1; 6; XXIV, 10; XXVII, 16.

22. יפריחו, intransitive Hiph'il (similarly, Job xiv, 9), refers here to the
"trees by the water".

23. טרם, of the previous line, is to be applied here. Similarly, Ps. xc, 2.

24. The greater part of the *beth* and a small part of the ascender of the *lamedh* are visible.

25. For the Pi'el here and in line 16 rather than the Qal, cf. Jer. xvii, 8.

26. Viz., the נצר of line 6.

27. Note the deviation from Job xxix, 19, whence it is obviously drawn. Targ. has here מבועא מיא. Is it a rendering of a text which had מים חיים (cf. Targ. on Gen. xxvi, 19; Lev. xiv, 5; 6; 50; Jer. ii, 13; Zech. xiv, 8)?

28. *Waw* dittographic.

29. Cf. Prov. x, 25. The V⁻ קור seems to be treated here as קרה, "furnish with beams". (Cf. מקרה, "beam work", Ec. x, 18). Qimḥi (QSS, p. 454), quoting his father, takes קורות (Cant. i, 17) from קור. The LXX and the Vulgate, on the other hand, seem to take קרתי (Is. xxxvii, 25) (1QIa קראתי!) from קרה, connecting it with the *wood* of the various trees mentioned in the preceding verse. (See Tur-Sinai, BI, pp. 2864-5). Again מקרה (לילה) (Deut. xxiii, 11) seems to be taken in 1QW as if belonging to קור (see YM, p. 302). In Aram., מקורייהו (איתי לי) (Bab. Qama 92b) appears to mean ("bring me) their *roots*" (see Rashi *ad hoc*). I. Wartski has drawn my attention to Tan. Buber, Gen. v, 38, p. 108, where מקורתו means "from his family" and to Yer. Soṭah 21b, where מקראי (Is. xlviii, 12) = תקרתי.

30. A lit. translation is "... the branch of its leaves" which may imply "its leaved-branch", hence "its foliage". However, since the whole line in which the last phrase is embodied is strongly influenced by Ez. xvii, 22-23 (note especially" ... in the *shadow* of the branches thereof"), נצר may mean here "concealed place", for which cf. ובנצורים ילינו (Is. lxv, 4). Hence my rendering. בנצר עליו may also be taken as בעלי נצרו. For similar syntactical anomalies, cf. line 87; 1QH, XXXVI, 10; XXXIX, 33. Cf. also 1QW, XXIX, 7.

31. For the possible R, cf. Ps. civ, 20. I have, however, restored חיות, not חיתו, as a trace of a letter, which is distinctly the tittle of the *taw*, is visible. Note that both חיתו of Is. lvi, 9 become חיות in 1QIa.

32. Or, taking מרמס in the construct state, "and the trampling (or treading) of its place became (a place) for...". As to גיזע (which occurs in lines 52 and 56 without a vocalic letter after the *gimel*), one wonders if it should not read גוזע, as a *yodh* does not seem to appear in the Scrolls in syllables such as the one under question. Examples of nouns considered to belong, according to the Masoretic pointing, to the *qatl* or *qitl* class appear numerously in 1QIa with *waw* after the first radical (indicating the *qotl* class?). Cf. e.g. XII, 20; XVI, 21; 22; XXVIII, 4; XXXIX, 4; XL, 1; XLV, 4; 5; LIII, 28 (wrongly transcribed). Cf. also 1QS, VII, 13;

XI, 22 (see n. 248); 1Q, p. 110, col. I, 19, where פותי‎=פתי‎ (contrast RZD, XIII, 6); RZD, XIII, 11, where שוכלו‎=שכלו‎. (Habermann, 'Edhah we- 'Eduth, p. 118, line 5, שיכלו‎). (Are the segholate nouns in ZPY, pp. 10, 4; 15, 97 and 192, 7 relics of this type of spelling? The editor takes the vocalic letter following the second radical in those three instances as a *yodh*. And again, is there a reflection of these forms in "Do not read בגדיו‎ (Gen. xxvii, 27) but בוגדיו‎" (Sanhedrin 37a)?). See n. 133.

33. Note the non-*plena*. As a rule, this word has a vocalic *waw* in the various writings of the Scrolls except in that of 1QIb.

34. For the last three lines, cf. Ez. xxxi, 6; 13; and Dan. iv, 8-9. Cf. also 1QH, XL, 15-17 and see the suggested RR of their *lacunae* in WHR, pp. 247-8.

35. For the form, cf. Ez. x, 15.

36. See n. 15.

37. See n. 19. For the force of *beth*, see n. 12.

38. For meaning, cf. Is. xvii, 11, where its Pilpel form is parallel with תפריחי‎. For the form, cf. Jer. xlix, 3. Cf. also WHR, p. 249, line 148 and see corresponding n. 5, p. 262.

39. The *waw* in this circumstantial clause introduces here a statement of the concomitant conditions. For similar uses of the *waw*, cf. Gen. xviii, 27; xlviii, 14.

40. See n. 25.

41. Used here intransitively, for the reference here is to נצר‎, that follows it. See n. 22.

42. Parts of the main body of the *koph* and the roof of the *daleth* are intact.

43. See n. 19. For some echo of the phrase, cf. Jer. ii, 21; Ps. lxxxv, 12.

44. For space after this word, see n. 10. Here, however, it is more likely due to the first reason mentioned in the note. For Pu'al of סתר‎, cf. Prov. xxvii, 5. For idea of last line, cf. line 6. Cf. also 1QH, XXXIX, 11; 26.

45. כלוא‎ (= כלא‎) followed by the perfect is peculiar to the Hymns (cf. e.g. lines 19; 27; 28; 1QH, XLVI, 34). Cf., however, Gen. xxxi, 20. Cf. also Lam. iv, 14, where it is followed by the imperfect.

46. For the phrase with the *beth* of the first word omitted, cf. I Kings x, 21.

47. See n. 45.

48. There is here a space capable of containing about five letters. See n. 10. Here, however, it seems to be due to the end of the section. For some echo of the last line, cf. perhaps Nah. iii, 17. Cf. also Dan. xii, 4; 9. See n. 13.

49. Very common in the Hymns (cf. e.g., 1QH, XXXIX, 11; 14; 32; XL, 20. Cf. also further line 32.) Hence R.

50. Rather than שַׁבִּיתָה; cf. Job i, 10.

    גבורי כוח (phrase not found in the Bible in the *plena*), "angels of might", is suggested by its parallel in line 22. Cf. Ps. ciii, 20. Cf. also "angel of might" (Test. Jud. iii, 10); גבורי שמים (1QH, XXXVII, 35-36); [ג]בורי אלים and גבורים (YM, p. 210, where the references to 1QW are given). For "secrets of angels", cf. I En. lxv, 6. For··· גבור··· ברז, cf. גבור···פלא (Is. ix, 5).

52. רוחות denoting angels is very common in the Scrolls as well as in the Apocryphal literature (see YM, p. 211). See following n.

53. O מתהפכת - a misprint. (For the pausal form, cf. the Masoretic pointing of נהפכת, Jonah iii, 4). For the whole line, cf. Gen. iii, 24, where חרב comes instead of אש. See, however, Targ. Yer. on Gen. iii, 24. Cf. II En. xxx, 1, where armed angels of *fire* guard "the Garden". So apparently also according to Mid. Rab. (end of s. 21).

54. An impersonal verb, referring to other than the נצר mentioned in lines 6 and 17. This indefinite personal subject repeats itself in lines 25, 26, 27 and 28. Impersonal verbs are not uncommon in the Bible. Cf. e.g. Gen. xi, 9; Is. viii, 4; Mi. ii, 4.

55. This possible R is based on its parallel phrase of line 25.

56. A good part of the *mem* is visible.

57. This expression (not found in this form in the Bible) seems to be here elliptical for מעין עצי חיים, referred to in line 6. Hence my translation. See following nn. However, חיים qualifying [ממי is also a possibility.

58. This seems to be an equivalent of עצי חיים which produce the עולם···נצר (see line 6).

59. Elliptical for ···נצר קודש, mentioned in line 17, the water being that of the "secret fount" (see n. 13). The greater part of the last two lines are to be found in 1Q, p. 137, 2.

60. The leg of the *resh* appears to be visible.

61. A metaphor for the "everlasting" and "holy" נצר referred to above. The hymnologist's thanks to God for placing him in the "congregation of the children of heaven" mentioned in 1QH, XXXVII, 21-22 deserves attention here.

62. For this word and its counterpart in line 28, see n. 45.

63. Cf. Deut. xxxiii, 9 and Is. vi, 10.

64. For this preposition — ל rather than ···ב — following האמן which implies expectation etc., cf. Is. liii, 1; Ps. xxvii, 13.

65. Lit. "a stem of life". For this rendering, see n. 29, and cf. עצי חיים (line 6).

66. = אשר יתן.

67. A number of restored nouns, containing the V‾ פרח (justified, more or less, on paleographical as well as on morphological grounds), suggest themselves here. However, the one restored — a noun on the pattern of יצהר ("oil") — seems to be the most likely. The space between the *yodh* and the (damaged) *resh* is admittedly too large for the size of one letter, but this may be due to the piece of parchment moved unduly slightly to the left. See following n.

68. Cf. line 6 with special reference to למטעת עולם. Cf. also 1QH, XL, 15 and see n. 20.

69. A dot follows the *lamedh*, after which comes a space capable of containing one letter. This is followed by זאי. Taking into consideration the word נהרות that follows it, which brings at once to one's mind Is. xviii, 2; 7, I have restored ל[כ]זאי (cf. 1QIa which distinctly reads in both 2 and 7 בזאי. (So KK. Burrows, erroneously, בזאו)), a noun the pattern of which is common in the Talmudic literature. Cf. e.g. גנאי and תנאי where the *'aleph* is, as in our case, vocalic. For *'aleph* as indicating the equivalent of the *qamez* (?) in the Scrolls, cf., perhaps, 1QIa, I, 19; 26; 1QH, XXXIX, 21. For the contempt levelled against the hymologist, cf. line 170 and see nn. thereon.

70. The first copyist made it run together with its preceding word. A later hand, however, apparently realizing the absurdity of this combination, attempted to erase the *nun* and added one dot above it and another below it to indicate elision and superposed a *nun* of his own (note its shape which differs from that of other *nuns* in the MS.) meant to be drawn to הרות. See V.T., VII, 2 (1957), pp. 211-212.

71. Cf. Jer. xlvii, 2.

72. כי is often taken in the Hymns in the sense of "indeed", "yea", "surely".

73. Cf. Is. lvii, 20. For the last two lines, cf. "And I was (the subject of a derisive) song to transgressors . . ., roaring like gales (on the high) seas when their waves are stirred up, (and) casting up mire and mud" (1QH, XXXVI, 11-13).

74. See n. 49.

75. Cf. Is. li, 16.

76. For this possible R, cf. 1QH, XXXVIII, 24; XXXIX, 9. See V.T., V, 3, p. 280, n. 9.

77. Cf. lines 2-4.

78. = . . . אשר לא. See n. 66. For the whole line, cf. "and thou shalt be like

a . . . spring of water, whose waters fail not" (Is. lviii, 11). Cf. also John iv, 14.

79. For a somewhat similar use of the infinitive, cf. להפריח (line 6) and להשריש (line 7) and see their respective nn.

80. The more obvious R is השמ]ים (Cf. Is. xxiv, 18; Ps. lxxviii, 23; Mal. iii, 10. Cf. also מקור אשר ל]וא יכז]ב יפתח לך מן השמים ...1Q, p. 120, 3-4). However, the relic of the third letter visible is not that of a *mem*. Moreover, . . . ויהיו לנחל (line 36) would not tally with "the heavens". I therefore restore, hesitatingly, השק]ים, "the springs (of water)" (Targum's rendering of גלת, Jud. i, 15, is בית שקיא), for which cf. "the fountains of the great deep were broken up" (Gen. vii, 11a). Cf. also Zech. xiii, 1, For the last four lines, cf. 1QH, XXXVI, 17-18.

81. The *waw*, slightly damaged, and not recorded in O, is superposed between the final *mem* of the preceding word and the *lamedh*.

82. Apparently elliptical for ולא ימישו מ . . . . The possibility of the reading of ימושו, in the Qal, thus changing the meaning of the whole line, can not be ruled out. For the last two lines, cf. 1Q, p. 120, 3-4.

83. See n. 71.

84. This possible R, not too big to be comprised by the lacuna, is suggested by the context. Similar RR, however, suggest themselves here.

85. The *qoph*, not recorded in O, is only partly visible. This word might or might not have been followed by another word, as there is no harmony in the position of words at the end of lines. See n. 10.

86. Perhaps פותאום (= פתע with terminal *mem*, and with *'ayin* weakened for *'aleph*) is to be read. See n. 32, where the spelling of a segholate noun similar to פתע is discussed. Cf. what seems to read רוקמה (1QW, XX, 6; 9; 14) (YM, ריקמה). See JSS, II, 3, p. 294.

87. For the Hiph'il of נבע not followed by the direct subject, cf. Ps. lix, 8.

88. See line 6 where we are told that "the secret fount" is hidden (along with the "trees of life").

89. Leg of first *waw* damaged.

90. The medial *mem* and the *yodh* are split into two parts, due to a tear in the MS.

91. A possible R. Cf. Jud. v, 21.

92. Elliptical for עץ לח . . . . Cf. Ez. xxi, 3. Cf. also "and torrents . . . will overflow . . ., so as to consume every green and withered tree" (1QH, XXXVII, 29-30).

93. A noun from צלל; cf. חרש מצל, "a shadowing wood" (Ez. xxxi, 3). Cf. also perhaps מצלות (Zech. xiv, 20) which, according to some mediaeval

commentators (e.g. Ḥayyuge and Janaḥ). (Cf. R. Yehoshuʻa b. Levi's opinion, Pesaḥim 50a), is connected with צלל, "shadow".

94. A possible R. See following n. In order to get some sense out of this seemingly out-of-key metaphor, I have restored a Hiphʻil rather than a Qal — though the Hiphʻil exists only in the post-Biblical literature. Cf. ירדו במצולות (Ex. xv, 5), הצלילם...כמו אבן (Mid. Wayyoshʻa, Yelinek, i, 46). The Hiphʻil of צלל is used extensively in payṭanic compositions.

95. Cf. Ex. xv, 10.

96. The last letter of this word and all the letters of the preceding word are hardly visible, but my suggested reading may perhaps be justified by Am. iv, 10; Joel ii, 20; Is. xxxiv, 3. Cf. also יהפכו כעצי באושים (line 59). Another reading, and more obvious at that, is תאכלם אש, but in this case it would be hard to explain ויבשו, for the reference seems to be, according to lines 39-40, to trees etc.

97. The *yodh* is superposed.

98. Elliptical for פרי עץ (Gen. i, 11). For a similar ellipsis, see n. 92.

99. For likely R, cf. line 6. The *ẓadê* of the last word is not clear.

100. (The *resh* slightly damaged) = ופאר. Cf. ופארי = ופרי (1QW, XXII, 11). The omission of a radical guttural is not uncommon in the Scrolls, (cf. e.g. 1QIa, XXII, 19; XXXI, 8; XXXIII, 11) and to a lesser extent in the M.T. A similar case to ours is perhaps פארור = פרור (Num. xi, 8; contrast Joel ii, 6). For meaning, cf. Is. iii, 20. But perhaps it is to be taken in the sense of "bough", for which cf. third word of line 49.

101. A possible R. Cf. Is. lxi, 3.

102. The reference is apparently to the "trees of life". Cf. line 61; 1QH, LII, 10; 12. In Zech. xiii, 1 מקור נפתח refers to the House of David. Cf. 1QS, XI, 3; 5.

103. The *mem*, the shape of which differs from that of the other *mems* is superposed above the *pe*. I have vocalized the *lamedh* with *shewa* (and not with *pataḥ* as is למפלגות in II Ch. xxxv, 12), since the absolute form (which has here the apparent meaning of פלג, "a channel". Cf. מפלגיהם, 1QH, XXXVII, 30) seems to be here מפלג, on the *miqṭal* pattern — a pattern used as a rule as the form of infinitive Qal in Aram. and prevalent in the Scrolls in general and in 1QW in particular. It is interesting to note that מפלגיה in 1QW means "its divisions" (see YM, p. 320), and מפלגיהן which appears three times in 1QS, IV, 15-17, is parallel with דרכיהן of line 15. In 1QH, XLVI, 23 we have "and according to their rule they shall serve thee . . .] למפלג ". For my translation of עם, see n. 129.

104. For the use of the infinitive here, cf. Ez. xvii, 6.

105. Here and in the following line אל = על.

106. The force of לפנות of the preceding line is also to be applied here.

107. Rather than משקלת (for which cf. II Kings xxi, 13), for as a rule there is no paucity of vocalic letters in the Scrolls. For similar spelling, cf. 1QH, XL, 26.

108. A strange expression, a literary translation of which hardly yields any sense. The idea, however, becomes somewhat clearer by its parallel line 46. The plant, we seem to be told, will turn towards the place where the rays of the sun will not fall upon it vertically and directly so that it is not stricken by the intense heat thus emitted. For other functions of the sun, see I En. lxxii, 3 - lxxiii, 4; III Bar. vi, 1 - viii, 7; RZD, X, 15-16; 1Q, p. 105 (as reference to Hebrew text, p. 103, 6); 1QW, XXXIII, 5. For קו and משקלת, cf. Is. xxviii, 17 and II Kings xxi, 13.

109. For this possible R, cf. its contrast in line 42.

110. Masc. of כנה (Ps. lxxx, 16). For a similar possible case, cf. כנו (ועמד מנצר שרשיה) (Dan. xi, 7). In this connection, cf. also מנצר כנם עמדו (Saadyah Gaon in his Hebrew introduction to 'Egron).

111. Cf. the Masoretic pointing of this word in the absolute in Is. x, 33.

112. See n. 160. Expressions in which הנף is embodied occur in the Hymns numerous times. Cf. also 1QW, XXXII, 9.

113. The V‾עזק, which is a *hapax legomenon* in the Bible (Is. v, 2) in the Pi'el, appears not infrequently in post-Biblical Hebrew in the Qal.

114. = פלכיו. At first sight it looks like being a plural of the so-called *local extention* or *surface plural* of the type of שמים and מרחקים etc., but see n. 123. For the interchange of the *kaph* and *gimel* in the Scrolls, see 1Q, p. 129; 1QS, XI, 1. Cf. also אגזרי, instead of אכזרי (1QIa, XI, 18). See G. Dalman, *Grammatik des Jüdisch-Palestinischen Aramaisch*, p. 99. See also EMNM, p. 1226. In this connection, the noun פלג of the Umm-el-'Awamid inscription of 132 B.C. (see CNSI, p. 44, 3), which has the obvious meaning of "district", "border", is worthy of comparison. According to W. F. Albright, פלג, without equating it with פלך, means "furrow made by plough or hoe for the purpose either of planting seed or irrigating the ground".

115. Cf. Job viii, 16-17. In Deut. xxxii, 13, the last two words appear in a reversed order. See n. 30.

116. For this possible R, for which the lacuna is big enough, cf. Is. liii, 2; xl, 24.

117. A rendering of the common Biblical expression עצר כח. The line contains Jer. xvii, 8 in a condensed form.

118. For the opposite, see line 50.

119. The bigger part of the *waw* and part of the right stroke of the *'ayin* are visible. See following n.

120. The possible R, taking in consideration line 56 (for which see following n.), is based on Jer. xvii, 6. In Jer., however, the reading is ... כערער and not ... כערוער, but see BDB, where the probable latter reading is suggested on account of Jer. xlviii, 6.

121. The last two lines are obviously influenced by Jer. xvii, 6. Note the deviation and especially that of חרלים, instead of חררים.

122. See n. 114 as well as the following n.

123. The verb is rightly in the singular, as is the noun שרשיו of line 57, both of which govern פלגיו which is here a singular. It appears that the members of the Sect have most likely pronounced the suffix יו as o (so do the Samaritans; see Z. Ben-Ḥayyim, *Studies in the Tradition of the hebrew Language*, Madrid-Barcelona, 1954, pp. 79-82; see also YKS, in the Scrolls in general and in 1QIa in particular terminate in יו. Cf. e.g. 1QIa, XXIII 15; XXXIII 10; XXXV 13; XXXVIII 15; XLVIII 29; XLIX 2; LIV 3. Cf. perhaps also the *Nash Papyrus*, line 16. See V.T. VII, 2, pp. 209-211.

124. Cf. Gen. iii, 18; Is. xxxii, 13.

125. Cf. Is. vii, 23. For the R in the sing., cf. יעל and see n. 123.

126. For possible R of its preceding word, cf. line 6, which speaks about the נצר sprouting out of the "trees of life". The word שפתו, which according to accepted Hebrew usage is not applicable to trees, may refer to מעין רז at which the trees are situated. Cf. Ez. xlvii, 7; 12.

127. Lit. "stinking". Cf. line 42. For באושים, cf. Is. v, 4.

128. See n. 123, but, perhaps, read עליו (= עלהו) (cf. Ps. i, 3 and Ez. xlvii, 12, whence the phrase in which this word occurs is obviously drawn).

129. For possible R, cf. lines 9 and 45. The letters of מכור, except for the *mem*, are slightly impaired. Its meaning seems to be that of מקור (I. Wartski has drawn my attention to the spelling of כורה instead of קורה in a number of places in the Talmudic literature, e.g. Mid. Rab. (Theodor Albeck), p. 138; Yerushalmi 'Erubin 21a). Aquila in rendering מכרות(יהם) (Gen. xlix, 5) „ἀνασκαφαί" obviously connects it with כרה, "to dig" (hence, perhaps, "origin"). Cf. Gen. xxvi, 25, where it is applied to a well. For the translation of ... עם, cf. ... עם באר ... ("and Isaac dwelt) *beside* (or *close to*) the well ..." (Gen. xxv, 11).

130. For R, see the words that follow it and cf. Jer. vi, 25; xx, 3; 10; xlvi, 5;

Ps. xxxi, 14. Cf. also 1QH, XXXIX, 35. However, a verb such as מלאתי may also serve here as a possible R.

131. *Mem* damaged.

132. Only part of the *beth* is visible.

133. O בנגיעים. Cf. lines 129; 169; 1QH, LI, 8. Many of the segholates, however, which are considered, according to the Masoretic pointing, as belonging to the *qatl* or the *qotl* class, appear, apparently under Aramaic influence, in the Scrolls with *waw* after the second radical. Cf. e.g. כבשים = כבושים (1QIa, V, 17); שחר = שחור (ib. V, 24); עצם = עצום (1QW, XXVI, 5); הצדק = הצדוק (1QS, IX, 14); ישר = ישור (ib. IX, 2). (See WHR, p. 254, n. 6). Cf. perhaps also 1Q, p. 67, where the Masoretic גבר of Is. xxii, 17 becomes גבור. For a relic of this kind of spelling in the Bible, cf. perhaps the *kethibh* בטרום (Ruth iii, 14). The following examples from the Talmudic literature may also have a bearing on this spelling: "Do not read אחת (Num. vii, 43) but אחות" (Num. Rab. sec. 13, end); "... זרעם (Is. lxi, 9) but זרועם" (Pesiqta Rab. sec. 35); "... בשר זרעו (Is. ix, 19) but זרעו ..." (Sab. 33a). See A. M. Honeyman, "An Unnoticed Euphemism in Is. ix, 19-20", in V.T., vol. I, pp. 221-3. In the light of the above examples, זרוע of 1QIa may very likely equal זרע, "offspring". For the phrase, cf. I Kings viii, 38.

134. Following the *beth* there is a letter resembling a *yodh* or a *waw*. The line echoes Jer. xxiii, 9; and xiv, 9.

135. The *waw*, not recorded in O, is obscure.

136. O לי.

137. The *gimel* and 'ayin are partly damaged. For R of *waw* after the second radical, see n. 133. For expression, cf. Lev. xiii, 20.

138. Lit. "for bitterness". For the whole line and the use of the *lamedh*, cf. 1QH, XXXIX, 27 and WHR, p. 243, 24 and notes 8 and 9, p. 259. Cf. also 1QH, XXXIX, 32; 34; 1QPHab, LIX, col. ix, 11.

139. Or *kaph* with *qamez*(?) O כאיב, but see WHR, p. 244, n. 1 and p. 253, n. 12. See also n. 133.

140. Cf. Is. xvii, 11 and see preceding note.

141. Other RR suggest themselves here, amongst them worthy of mention is perhaps ו[לבי ישתומ[מה; cf. Ps. cxliii, 4, by which this and the following two lines are obviously influenced. Cf. aslo 1QH, XLI, 3; LII, 20 in different circumstances. The placing of *he* after *mem* at the end of words is a very common feature in 1QIa. In the Hymns it occurs twice, once in line 73 of the present hymn and again in XLVII, 10.

142. This line is interesting exegetically. It is obvious that במתים חפשי (Ps. lxxxviii, 6), which is usually translated "free among the dead", and

ותחפש רוחי (Ps. lxxvii, 7), the accepted translation of which is "and my spirit made (delight) search", are here at play. The hymnologist, however, seems to have taken חפש of both Ps. lxxxviii, 6 and lxxvii, 7 as being identical. Taking into account this possibility as well as the context, I have translated freely "adrift", a rendering which may have part of the connotation of both חפש and חפש. I have, however. left it unvocalized, indicating that it suffers two ways of pointing.

143. For possible R, cf. Ps. lxxxviii, 4.

144. For possible R, see the two words that follow it and cf. Ps. cxliii, 4.

145. Cf. Jer. xiv, 17.

146. The subject matter is here נגוע, mentioned in line 66, where the verb פרח is applied. Such a come-back to a subject after having dealt with other subjects, due to thinking driven by emotion, is not uncommon in the Hymns, and it is much in evidence in the present hymn.

147. For R, cf. Jer. xx, 9. Note that אש here, unlike that of Jer., is governed *twice* by verbs indicating the masc.

148. For the morphology, see n. 141. For my free rendering, cf., perhaps, Jer. li, 42 and Lam. ii, 13, where the sing. is used figuratively.

149. Cf. Job xxxi, 12 and Deut. xxxii, 22. Cf. also 1QH, XXXVII, 31.

150. (Part of the *beth* damaged) = שלהבתה . There is no similar clear case in the Bible where the radical *he* loses its consonantal sound in the middle of a word. For a clear case in early (?) post-Biblical Hebrew, see S. Lieberman, *Tosephoth Rishonim* (1937), p 148. For the gender of אש, see n. 147.

151. קץ and מועד of the last two lines — terms which occur extensively in the Scrolls (see YM, pp. 234-235; 239-240) as well as in Dan. — have an apocalyptic sense, denoting a fixed period or epoch. Here the hymnologist, who appears to be living at the time of the writing of his hymn in the Evil Period which is due according to his belief to expire at a certain preordained time, expresses anxiety lest he be exhausted before the commencement of the Good Period. In this connection, הקץ האחרון 1QPHab, LVIII, col. vii, 7 and 12) is of special interest here. Cf. also גמר הקץ (ib., 2). For linguistic allusions, cf. Dan. viii, 23-24; ix, 24; Is. x, 18.

152. O records this word in full.

153. The preceding word, not recorded in O, is severely damaged. However, the traces left of its letters as well as phrases elsewhere in the Hymns (cf. e.g. 1QH, XXXVII, 16; 27) which also serve as a guide in the rendering of משברים in this context, suggest this reading. Cf. also Ps. xci, 5.

154. Cf. Ps. xlii, 6; 7; 12; xliii, 5. כלה is a favourite in the Hymns. For its adverbial usage, cf. II Ch. xii, 12; 1QH, XL, 32; XLI, 4.

155. Cf. Ez. xxx, 18, מעוזי, however, being a favourite in the present hymn. Cf. the first Hebrew word in 1Q, p. 137 (which is part of a hymn resembling that of ours) and ib., p. 106, fragment 4, where we have [עוז שבת].... The word מעוז, which is as a rule parallel in the Bible with מבצר, may be due here to its association with Is. xvii, 3.

156. Cf. II Sam. xiv, 14, and Jos. vii, 5.

157. Cf. Ps. xxii, 15. For the last two lines, cf. also 1QH, XXXVIII, 33-34.

158. Cf. Is. xxi, 3; Nah. ii, 11. I have translated "to nought", which has something of the original meaning connoting sudden terror or ruin.

159. *Mem* damaged. For the whole line,, cf. Job xxxi, 22. The יה-ending is a favourite in the Hymns. Cf. e.g. XLI, 2 (where almost an identical phrase is to be found); XXXVII, 8; 9; 10; 12; 18; XL, 27 and further line 186 in the present hymn. Cf. also 1QW, XIX, 2 and RZD, XIII, 1. See WHR, p. 264, n. 1.

160. A common Biblical expression. See line 50.

161. The first three letters are hardly visible. For R, cf. Ps. ix, 16. See n. 163.

162. = נלכדה, the error due to *homoioteleuton,* the eye of the copyist having wandered to the word that follows it which begins with *beth.*

163. Cf. Ps. cxlix, 8; cv, 18; Job xxxvi, 8. Cf. also 1QH, XXXIX, 37.

164. Cf. Ez. vii, 17. The treatment of fem. as masc. is a common practice in the Mishnah in similar instances.

165. Cf. the common Biblical שלח יד. Cf. also Job xxx, 12.

166. The first two letters are damaged.

167. = קול למצער ... (See n. 30). Cf., however, I Kings xiv, 6. Note the preference given here and in lines 88 and 194 to מצער rather than to the more common and equally Biblical צער, מצער being on the *miqtal* pattern, which is a favourite in the Scrolls. See n. 103. מצער is also used in 1QH, XXXVI, 18; 23; 33; XXXVII, 17; 25.

168. All the letters of the last two words are heavily crabbed, but the phrase that follows them serves here as a guide. See n. 170.

169. The first two letters are damaged.

170. For the last three words, cf. Nah. iii, 10 as well as line 95 further in the hymn. Cf. also line 84 and see n. 163.

171. First *he* somewhat faint. אשר הגברתה = הגברתה. For expression, cf. Ps. xii, 5.

172. *Yodh* not clear.

173. = כלה. *Lamedh-he* verbs following the analogy of *lamedh-'aleph* verbs is not uncommon in the Scrolls as well as in the Bible. As to this

particular verb, cf. on the one hand בלוי (Jer. xxxviii, 11) and on the
other hand בלואי (xxxviii, 12). Cf. also "Do not read בלא עם (Deut.
xxxii, 21) but בלוי עם (Siphri Wa'ethḥannan, 21). For לשון as masc.,
cf. Job xxvii, 4; Lam. iv, 4; Ps. xxii, 16. For nouns used as both masc.
and fem. in the same sentence, cf. Gen. xxxiii, 9; I Kings xix, 11; Jer.
xx, 9. For the phrase, cf. Zech. xiv, 12. בלה applied to lips is common
in the Talmudic literature. Cf. e.g. יבלו שפתותיכם (Sab. 32b) as reference
to Mal. iii, 10. The taking of ברא in the sense it has in lines 27 and 28
is also a possibility, but in this case ingenuity would be rather taxed to
explain line 90.

174.   נאספה ... may have some bearing on Jer. xlvii, 6, where the reference
is to a sword stopping to function on account of putting itself up in a
scabbard. If so, we will have to understand נאספה as an ellipsis.

175.   *Resh* damaged. For the line in which this word is embodied, cf., among
other verses in the Bible, Is. xxxvii, 23.

176.   *Waw* damaged. This and the word that follows it bring to mind Is. 1, 4.
Hence possible R.

177.   The two *mems,* the second of which not recorded in O, are damaged.

178.   = להחיות. Similar elisions of *hes* are not uncommon in the M.T. Cf.
e.g. Is. xxix, 15; Jer. xxxvii, 12; Ps. xxvi, 7. It is interesting to note
that this very word appears twice in 1QIa, XLVII, 16 with *he* elided.

179.   = לעיף. For consonantal *yodhs* turning into consonantal *'alephs* in the
M.T., cf., perhaps, Mi. vi, 10; Is. li, 19 (1QIa, ינחמך!). The *'ayin waw*
forms found in Ez. xxviii, 24; Jud. iv, 21 may also be of interest here,
and following the Masoretic pointing we may point here לְעָאֵף.

180.   The last two lines are made up, with some deviations, of Is. 1, 4, the
less slight of which is the substitution of להחיות רוח כושלים (for which
cf. Is. lvii, 15. See n. 178) for לדעת. Cf. also 1QH, XLI, 10. As to
the translation of לעות, I have followed the meaning given it in the
Jewish tradition which is illustrated by Targ. and by mediaeval as well
as by modern Hebrew writers.

181.   Word damaged. O כול, doubting *kaph.*

182.   Word damaged. For the whole line, cf. Ps. xxxix, 10.

183.   The first two letters, not recorded in O, are damaged. For R, see the
words that follow it and cf. Ps. cxlix, 8 and 9 with special reference to
משפט (see n. 224). Another possible R is ות]רותק, for which see line 88.

184.   Cf. line 88 and see n. 224.

185.   The last two letters, which are rather crabbed, are not recorded in O.

186. For a similar doubling of words, followed by a participle, cf. Lam. i, 16.

187. Part of what seems to be a *he* is visible. For the phrase, cf. Deut. xi, 16; Job xxxi, 9.

188. The last three letters, not recorded in O, are partly damaged. For the whole preceding line along with קירו[תיו, cf. מעי מעי ... קירות לבי .. לבי (Jer. vii, 19).

189. For the pointing of this word, cf. Lam. iii, 15. See n. 138.

190. For possible R, read the whole line and cf. Prov. i, 6, but here להבין is used transitively. Cf. 1QS, VI, 15. Cf. also Ec. xii, 9. For similar constructions, cf. lines 83; 86; 91. See following two notes.

191. Cf. Is. xxxvi, 4, but here נמהרים is used in the good sense, referring apparently to the members of the Sect. Cf. 1QH, XXXV, 35; XXXVI, 9; XXXIX, 22; 1QS, X, 26 and WHR, p. 252, n. 1.

192. ═ משל lit. "proverb", "parable". Cf. Sanhedrin 38b: "Rabbi Meir knew three hundred ממשלות", the sing. being either מֶמְשָׁלָה (or first *mem* with *ḥireq*), or מָמְשָׁל, both forms of which are found in the Bible with a sense other than given it here. For preference given in the Scrolls to the *miqtal* pattern, see nn. 103 and 167. For the last line, cf. ולהבין פותאים בכוח גבורתך ...ולהבין אנוש חקר (1QH, LVI, fragment 15).

193. Here come two indistinct letters.

194. The *lamedh*, only the ascender of which is visible, is not recorded in O.

195. The *taw*, not recorded in O, is only partly visible.

196. Cf. Ec. viii, 16. Hence possible RR in the beginning of the line.

197. Here come a few indecipherable letters.

198. Word damaged owing to a tear in the MS. Tears of a similar nature occur in רחמים, where the *mem* is split perpendicularly into two parts, and in קנאה (line 106), where the *qoph* is split in the same way.

199. Cf. Is. xlii, 13. But does "he" here refer to a certain personality plotting against the hymnologist? See WHR, p. 252, n. 5 and further in the present hymn, lines 123-125; 157; 160-161.

200. The base of the *kaph* slightly faint. For the last two lines, cf. Ez. v, 13. Cf. also Ez. xiii, 13, where לכלה is used, as the case is also here, adverbially. Cf. also 1QPHab, LX, col. xii, 5 (if its preceding words are to be translated "whom God will *punish*". See n. 222).

201. For the possible R, for which the lacuna is big enough, see the words that follow it and cf. II Sam. xxii, 5. However, other RR, amongst them involving the rearrangement of the last two lines, suggest themselves.

202. ═ ערש יצועי, for which cf. Ps. cxxxii, 3. Cf. also משכב יצועי (1QS, X, 14). The reversion of the order of words is a characteristic feature in

the Hymns. See n. 30. For the whole line, cf. Job xvii, 13 and Ps. cxxxix, 8.

203. Rather than [מ]שכבי, for a fem. noun is required here. Cf. Job vii, 13 and Ps. vi, 6.

204. *Beth* slightly faint.

205. For Biblical references, see n. 203.

206. Cf. . . . ותמס כעש "and . . . melted (or consumed) away like a moth" (Ps. xxxix, 12). Numerous other renderings, some of which based on emendation of the text, leap here to one's mind. The one worthy of consideration, however, is to take עש here as "pus", connecting it with the Arabic غتيث. See G. R. Driver, *Difficult words in the Hebrew Prophets* in *Studies in O.T. Prophecy*, pp. 66-67. The translation of the line in which this word is embodied will thus be "My eyes are like pus (produced) at a kiln", which, in addition to כבשן giving a better account of itself here, gives also a reasonable good parallel.

207. Cf. Lam. i, 16; ii, 11; iii, 49.

208. מנוח is a more common word in the Scrolls than מנוחה. Cf. e.g. 1QW, XVII, 9. For a Biblical echo, cf. Ps. cxix, 123.

209. The line in which it is embodied as well as the line that follows it echo strongly Ps. xxxviii, 12. Hence possible R. See n. 211.

210. The *yodh*, not recorded in O, is only partly visible.

211. There is a small space between this word and its following one. See n. 10. והיי מצד, seems to be a paraphrase of וקרובי מרחוק (Ps. xxxviii, 12) of which the author was here undoubtedly aware. For my translation of חיי, cf. the Arabic حَىّ and I Sam. xviii, 18, where it is explained in the same verse by the gloss משפחת אבי. See DBS, p. 153. See also n. 230.

212. The 'aleph of the first syllable is singled out for elision by dots placed one above it and one below it. This is in keeping with the style of the two parallel lines that follow it. For the expression, cf. Zeph. i, 15; Job xxx, 3; xxxviii, 27.

213. The first two letters are damaged. For expression, cf. II Ch. vi, 29.

214. Cf. II Sam. xxii, 5-6. For the last three lines, cf. "Calamity follows on calamity, and wound on wound, and tribulation on tribulation . . . and illness on illness" (Jub. xxiii, 13). Cf. also Is. liii, 4.

215. Cf. Ps. ix, 2; lxxi, 17; lv, 2; lxix, 27.

216. *He* damaged. For the line, cf. Gen. xxiv, 27; Ezra ix, 9.

217. = תשתעשע. For the omission of gutturals in the Scrolls, see n. 100. There is a space big enough to contain one letter between the second *taw* and the *shin* that follows it which may be due to a defect in the

parchment. (See n. 10.) Above the space there is a dot, placed apparently by a later hand, presumably bearing on the absence of the *'ayin*. For the *manner* of my pointing, cf. the similar Masoretic pointing in Jer. 1, 29. For the rendering of מקֵן לקֵן, see n. 151. See also V.T., IV, 2, pp. 211-212.

218. Cf. Ps. xciv, 19 and Is. lxiii, 15.

219. Cf. Ps. cxix, 42; Prov. xxvii, 11.

220. Apparently = למשתוחחי. O למשתוחחי. (An Aramaic influence? Cf. חזיר = חויר, 1QIa, LII, 1. See YKS, p. 169). Because of the uncertainty in the reading of this word I have left its last few letters unvocalized. The Hithpolel here has the force of the Hiph'il in ישיחו בי (Ps. lxix, 12) by which our phrase is influenced. Hence my translation. See line 162.

221. Cf. Hab. ii, 1.

222. For the last two lines, cf. Deut. xxv, 1.

223. For expression, cf. Is. xxxviii, 19. For ידע followed by *beth* cf. I Sam. xxii, 15; Ps. xxxi, 8.

224. במשפטי here seems to be parallel with ובנגועי (line 129). See line 95, and parallel its last two words with the last words of line 88. See also line 188. W. H. Brownlee is right in noting that ... במשפט ... in 1QS, VII, 8 is parallel with בתוכחת... of VI, 1 (see BASOR, Supplementary Studies, Nos, 10-12, p. 29, n. 18). See also G. S. Glanzman, "Sectarian Psalms...", in *Theological Studies*, XIII, 4, p. 513, n. 31. Cf. the V⁻ שפט in Ez. vii, 3 and xviii, 30.

225. See n. 133.

226. The last two lines which speak of the desire for suffering are not an isolated case in the Hymns. It is, however, here and elsewhere in the present hymn (e.g. lines 168-171) that it is so explicitly expressed. For submission in suffering in the O.T. and the N.T. as well as in the Talmudic literature, see H. H. Rowley, *Submission in Suffering,* (Cardiff, 1951), pp. 1-4; 10-12; 50-51; 59-66; 70-72. See also J. A. Sanders, *Suffering as Divine Discipline in the O.T. and P. B. Judaism* (New-York, 1955).

227. Cf. Ps. xliii, 8; cxix, 74; 81.

228. Letters, except for the *waw*, damaged.

229. The hymnologist, in keeping with the snatchy way in which he expresses now here and now there his religious beliefs (see J. Licht, "The Doctrine etc.", IEJ, VI, 1, p. 2), has thrown out here-another detail, namely, that to God is also to be attributed his capacity for prayer. For God putting a word or words into the mouth of men, cf. Num. xxiii, 5; Is. li, 16; lix, 21; Jer. i, 9. The translation "and thou hast given grace (or

"favour") in etc." is also tenable, thus echoing "grace is poured into thy lips" (Ps. xlv, 3) as well as Prov. x, 12; xxii, 11.

230. (גרעת = גערתה?). For a similar meaning of גערתה, cf. perhaps Ps. ix, 6, where it is parallel with אבדת and מָחִיתָ (see Ibn Ezra *ad hoc,* where he says that גערת not followed by *beth* implies "destruction" (כריתה. So QSS, גער ⁻V. Cf. perhaps also Rashi). For חיים "maintenance", cf. Prov. xxvii, 27. Cf. also מחיה, "sustenance". However, חיי may have here the meaning of חיתי, for which cf. Job xxxiii, 18; 20; 22; Ps. cxliii, 3; Ben Sira li, 6, where it is invariably parallel with נפש (It is also often used in this sense in Mediaeval Hebrew poetry of the Spanish School and to a lesser extent in piyyut. See ZPY, p. 12, 8.), and here would serve as a tolerably good parallel with שלומי of line 133. If so, we will have to translate "Not rebuking my soul". The translation "Not rebuking my companion" (or "my kinsfolk"), the reference being to the members of the Sect, looks here equally plausible (though the parallel would seem to be impaired). Cf. גער חית קנה (Ps. lxviii, 31), where חית is parallel with עדת. Cf. also II Sam. xxiii, 13 and see n. 211.

231. Cf. Jer. xvi, 5.

232. *Beth* damaged.

233. Cf. Ps. ix, 11.

234. There is a small space between this word and its following one. For the phrase, cf. Ps. cvii, 25, but here the Hiph'il of עמד has the meaning given it in Prov. xxix, 4, this being parallel with יסרתה (line 136). Cf. ... חזוק מעמד החזיקה במעמד לפני נגע (1QH, XXXVIII, 36). Cf. also (1QW, XXIX, 6).

235. Cf. Ps. viii, 3.

236. *Waw* partly faded.

237. Cf. Ps. xciv, 11. For meaning here, cf. Prov. i, 4; iii, 21; 1QH, XXXVIII, 21.

238. Cf. Jer. xxxi, 3 and Ps. cxix, 50.

239. *Beth* damaged.

240. Modelled after Ps. cxix, 16; 45. For ... סליחות, see n. 315.

241. This reference to what seems to be the Fall of Adam, a theme well developed in the N.T. and Apocrypha as well as in Jewish mystical works, is of special interest. The fact that it appears here in a casual and snatchy way (see n. 229) tends to show that this notion was sufficiently known to the hymnologist's followers, and thus not requiring elaboration. For a Biblical echo to the wording, cf. Is. xliii, 27. (According to Qimḥi, ראשון = Adam). Elsewhere in the Hymns we have פשעי ראשונים (1QH, LI, 18), which may refer to both Adam and Eve.

Cf., howover, Ps. lxxix, 8 and Jer. xi, 10. For a recent contribution on the fall of man, see Bo Reicke, *The Knowledge hidden in the Tree of Paradise*, JSS, I, 3, pp. 193-201.

242. *Daleth* of the first word and both letters of the second word are damaged.

243. Cf. Ez. x, 2; Ps. xiii, 6.

244. תוחלת = . Cf. תוכחה and תוכחת.

245. Cf. Is. li, 5; Job xxxix, 11.

246. (*Mem* damaged). Lit., "in thy judgement". See following n.

247. (*Yodh* superposed). Lit. "in thy dispute". The lines that follow, however, as well as Job xv, 14, xxv, 4; Ps. cxliii, 2, of which the author seems to have been mindful, suggest my rendering.

248. The rythem of this line is in keeping with neither its preceding lines nor with its succeding one. If we have here a *homoioteleuton*, it is possible that the original had ובשר מיצר בשר יחזק ויצר מיצר יכבד. For the translation of יצר, cf. Is. xxix, 16, where it is thus used emblematically. Cf. also ויוצר יד (= . . . ויצר. See n. 32) (1QS, XI, 22).

249. See following n.

250. In the last four lines we have again one of the Sect's notions known to us especially from 1QS, V, 21-24 and VI. Cf. also כפי נחלת איש באמת וצדק (ib. IV, 25); 1QH, XLVI, 22-23; cf. also XLVIII, 13, 18-20; LVI, fragments 10 and 11; 1Q, p. 110, col. I, 17-19, (with special reference to יכבדו איש מרעהו); col. II, 14-16; 21; RZD, XX, 4; 24. Cf. also En. xliii, 2, where if translated into a similar Hebrew to that of the hymnologist's would read כן יכבד אנוש מאנוש, (for the likelihood of Enoch having been written originally in Hebrew, see A. Kahana, *Ha-Sepharim ha-Ḥiẓoniyyin*, I, Tel-Aviv, 1937, p. 103). The verses that follow this one in Enoch remind one of lines 146-148 of our text. The idea of various grades allotted to men underlies perhaps also RDZ, VII, 4. For the metaphorical use of בשר, cf. Zech. ii, 17; Ez. xxi, 2. Cf. also 1QH, LV (fragment 5), 10; 1QW, XXVII, 12.

251. Last two letters not clear.

252. Cf. Deut. iii, 24. Cf. also 1QH, LII, 8.

253. A possible R in this context. The lacuna is also big enough to contain it and the restored letter that follows it. For אין קץ, cf. Ec. iv, 8; Is. ix, 6.

254. אין מדה does not exist in the Bible. For idea, however, cf. Is. xl, 13.

255. *Mem* damaged.

256. The *qoph* and *he* are not recorded in O. Their left parts are, however, visible enough. The middle letters are obscure. The RR in this line are in keeping with the context and style of the hymnologist in general and with that of the last few lines in particular. The word קצבה (cf. the

Biblical קצב) is very common in the Mishnah, where it is often followed by אין. It is also found in piyyuṭ.

For a possible R, cf. Deut. xxxi, 16 and Is. lvii, 21. For . . . נעזב מ, cf. נעזבתי מבריתכה (1QH, XXXVIII, 35). Cf. also נעזב מיראתו של הקב״ה (Mid. Rab. Lev. xxxv). The lacuna is capable of containing more than these two words, but part of the lacuna to the left does not seem to have contained any writing; the space preceding ואני proves it. (See n. 10).

258. This phrase is common in the Bible (cf. e.g. Gen. xxxii, 31; Jer. xx, 13; Ez. xiv, 14; Ps. lxxxvi, 13) and may serve as a possible R here.

259. The word that follows it suggests this possible R. Cf. Ps. xxiii, 4.

260. The *samech* is only partly visible. See following n.

261. For this possible R, cf. Ps. lxvi, 20; I Ch. xvii, 13. Other RR naturally suggest themselves here.

262. Here comes a word comprising three damaged and indecipherable letters.

263. = כאשר זומם לי. Cf. כוממ למו (1QH, XXXVIII, 26). Cf. also כאשר זמם לכלות אביונים (1QPHab, LX, col. xii, 6). For this anomalous construction (a very strong feature in piyyuṭ, beginning about the 6th cent. See M. Wallenstein, *Some Unpublished Piyyuṭim from the Cairo Genizah,* (Manchester, 1956) p. 45, n. 70; p. 49, n. 119), cf. Es. i, 10 and II Ch. i, 4. The verb here is an impersonal Po'al.

264. A possible R. For plotters against the hymnologist on the part of evil-doers, cf. especially 1QH, XXXVIII, 10-14. Cf. also ib. XXXVI, 16-17, where the V⁻ זמם is used. For צרי, rather than אויבי or שונאי, cf. line 160. Note also that the lacuna here would hardly contain a word comprising five letters in addition to the proposed restored words that follow it.

265. Only the tittle of the left part of the *he* and its leg are visible. For possible R, cf. lines 161-162. Cf. also Jer. iii, 25; Ps. xxxv, 26.

266. Cf. Dan. ix, 7; 8; 1QH, XXXVIII, 23. For אם...ואם, cf. Jer. xlii, 6; Ez. ii, 7.

267. Other RR leap to one's mind. For this possible R, however, cf. Ps. lxix, 14.

268. Cf. Lam. i, 16 and I Sam. xxv, 31.

269. Other possible RR are וריבי or ומצותי, for which cf. Is. xli, 11-12. Cf. also 1QH, XLI, 22-23.

270. Here is the end of the line after which there is a space big enough to contain about seven letters. (See n. 10). For the use of רגן in the Scrolls, see 1QH, XXXIX, 23; 1QS, XI, 1 (רוגנים = רוכנים). For similar unfamiliar construct states, cf. e.g. Ps. ii, 12; Jer. viii, 16. The Niph'al (rather than the Qal) seems to follow Is. xli, 11a of which the

last line looks its faithful paraphrase. Cf. perhaps also the peculiar first two words of line 124. Another R of the lacunae of the last few lines which would be more in keeping with the idea of submission in suffering mentioned above and enlarged on further in the hymn would be

וכזוםם לי ת[עשה לי אם לכלמ]ה ואם לבושת פנים ...

ואתה בר[ז חכמתכה] תגבר צרי עלי למכשול לי [ותבא את] אנשי

מלח[מתי לכסותני בו]שת פנים וכלמה לנרגני בי

but in this case the last words will be very hard to explain.

271. The *lamedh,* which is damaged, is superposed. The leg of the *yodh,* exept for its bottom point, is somewhat faint and the *waw* is obscure. The last two letters are not recorded in O.

272. Or הבראי. For these possible RR, cf. respectively Ps. cvi, 7 and Ez. xxviii, 15. For למיום, instead of מיום, cf. Jud. xix, 30; II Sam. vii, 6.

273. A common Biblical phrase. Cf. e.g. Jer. 1, 34; li, 36; Lam. iii, 58.

274. Common in the Scrolls. See YM, p. 241.

275. For בי rather than אותי, cf. Prov. xxx, 6.

276. The *'aleph* and part of the *mem* are faded.

277. For possible R, cf. 1QS, III, 15; 1Q, p. 136, 34, 1. Cf. also Is. xxxix, 8; Jer. xxxiii, 6. מועד as parallel to קץ is very common in the Scrolls. See n. 151.

278. Letters, except for final *mem,* damaged. O וששון. For the whole line, cf. Jer. xv, 16.

279. O ונגיעי.. See n. 133.

280. For possible R, cf. Jer. xxxiii, 6. For other possible RR, cf. Jer. xiv, 19; xxx, 13.

281. Cf. 1QH, XXXVI, 33; XXXVIII, 22. See n. 69.

282. For identical phrase, cf. 1QS, IV, 7. For reminicsences, cf. Is. xxviii, 5; lxii, 3; Jer. xiii, 18; Ez. xv, 12; Aboth iv, 13; Ben Sira xlv, 8 (with special reference to Aron); Test Ben. iv, 1; I Peter v, 4; Jewish liturgy for Sabbath morning, *Yismehu* (the same phrase as that of Ben Sira, but with reference to Moses). Cf. also 1Q, p. 124, 25; ib. p. 125 last line.

283. This line, at least in form, appears to be original. Cf. "... We glory in tribulation" (Romans v, 3); "... I wish my suffering" (above, line 129). The contents of the last seven lines so boldly and clearly expressed deserve attention. See nn. 226; 270.

284. For possible RR, cf. Dan. ix, 13; 22; 1QH, XLI, 26; XLV, 4; XLVI, 11-13; 33. Cf. also third benediction of *Shemoneh 'Esreh* prayer (see I. Elbogen, *Toledoth ha-Tephillah,* I, 1924, pp. 37-38).

285. Cf. Job xxxvii, 15; Is. lx, 1; 1QH, XXXVIII, 6; 23. For יפע in the Scrolls, cf. YM, p. 233.

286. The theme of light and darkness is a favourite with the Scrolls. In vocabulary the line brings to one's mind numerous passages occurring in the O.T., N.T. and Apocrypha as well as in Jewish liturgy. In form, however, it is peculiar.

287. For possible R, cf. Is. xxx, 26 in which the theme of light also referred to in lines 174-175, is mentioned.

288. Cf. lines 171. For גבורת פלא, cf. Is. ix, 5. Cf. also line 21.

289. A slender lacuna runs horizontally through this word, thus breaking it up, except for the *beth*, into two, and making it difficult to decipher. O does not record the *beth* and doubts the *resh*. For the morphology, see n. 133.

290. Top of the second letter is damaged and the third letter is indecipherable. O records them doubtfully as *pe* and *lamedh*. For the whole line, cf. Ps. iv, 2; cxviii, 5. For the last two words, cf. Gen. xlii, 21; Ps. xxxi, 8. Cf. also 1QH, XLIX, 16.

291. Part of the *mem* and almost the whole of the *nun* are missing.

292. *Waw* and *zayin* of the first word and *yodh* of the second word are damaged.

293. For the last four lines, cf. II Sam. xxii, 2-3; Jer. xvi, 19; Ps. lvii, 2.

294. The *kaph*, not recorded in O, is damaged.

295. There is here a space capable of containing about two letters (see n. 10). This line again recalls II Sa. xxii, 2-3. For the vocalization of לפלט, cf. Ps. xxxii, 7, but perhaps a segholate noun of the *qatl* class is to be preferred both here and in Ps. Cf. the proper noun פלט (I Ch. xii, 3). See line 193. Cf. 1QH, XXXVII, 28; XL, 25; LV, (fragment 2), 6.

296. Cf. Job viii, 12.

297. For this translation of ידעתני see D. W. Thomas, *Journal of Theol. Studies,* XXXVIII, p. 404. It is here in keeping with the notions expressed by the hymnologist intermittently in a number of lines of this hymn. It also appears to be a stylistic variation of line 188.

298. For the last two possible RR, cf. Ps. lxxi, 5-6. Other possible RR may be guided by Is. xlix, 1; Jer. i, 5; Ps. xxii, 10.

299. גמל על is a common Biblical expression, but its neighbourhood here with אמי is no doubt due to the influence of Ps. cxxxi, 2.

300. (First *waw* superposed) = הורתי parallel with אמי, for which cf. Cant. iii, 4 and Hos. ii, 7. O reads הורותי. For preference given in the Scrolls, and especially in the Hymns, for fem. nouns ending in ־יה, see n. 159.

301. Immediately preceding the line at the margin there are three dots thus ∴.

302. For the possible R, cf. 1QH, XLI, 21-22. Cf. perhaps also 1Q, p. 123, 23. Cf. also Prov. viii, 31. Another possible R is תכלכלני, for which

cf. line 201. The harping on a favourite word in sentences within a short distance from each other is a conspicuous feature in the Hymns. It is also in evidence in the hymn with which we deal.

303. Implying discipline and correction. See n. 224 and cf. line 183.

304. Cf. 1QH, LIII, (fragment 2), 15. I have taken נכון adverbially, אמת being fem. Cf. אל נכון (I Sam. xxiii, 23) and נכונה (Job xlii, 7; 8), both of which are adverbs. אמת נכון seems to be influenced by Deut. xiii, 15, where נכון, however, is an adjective qualifying the noun that follows it. For the line, cf. Ps. li, 11; 15. Cf. also Jud. xvi, 29.

305. The first word is obscure. So is the *qoph* of the second word. For the line, cf. Ps. cxliii, 10.

306. The letters in the square brackets are heavily damaged, out of which, however, the second looks like the bigger part of a *ḥeth*.

307. The ascender of the *lamedh* is faint. O records הל֗י [   ], taking the *he* of the preceding word as belonging here. For the line, cf. Jer. xii, 3 and Ps. xvii, 3.

308. The base of the *nun* as well as a slight part of its body are erased, and only part of the head of the first *waw* seems to be visible. O records ותי. For the line, cf. II Sam. vii, 4. Of special interest here are ... אוכיח כנעוותי ...; (כנעויתו ... (1QS, V, 24. Burrows, כנעוותו להוכיח ... (ib. X, 11. Burrows כנעויתי), נעורת being a noun from the V⁻ עוה with the Niph'al in mind (for which cf. Is. xxi, 3; Prov. xii, 8; Ben Sira xiii, 3; 1QH, XXXV, 22; XXXVII, 21; XLV, 12; XLVII, 15; LI, 19; LVI, fragment 12). For a noun of the intensive form, cf. עוורת (הדין) (Aboth v, 8). In the light of this suggested reading it is possible that the author read ... נעורת ... in the rather difficult I Sam. xx, 30 (note that the LXX reads ... נערת ...). For my translation of the V⁻ עוה, see DBS, p. 170, n. 2.

309. In the Mishnah משמר refers to a division for duty of priests and levites. Cf. Neh. xii, 24 and 1QW, XVII, 2-4.

310. Cf. משמרת שלום (in Grace after Meal, beginning *Bammarom*), which is usually rendered "enduring peace". Cf. also 1QH, LIII, (fragment 2), 5; LIV, (fragment 4), 5. Does our משמר שלום, however, allude to angels? Cf., perhaps, first Hebrew line of 1Q, p. 140 and 1QH, LII, 10 (end).

311. For pointing, see n. 295.
312. For the phrase, cf. Ps. xvii, 13.
313. The last three words are obscure in parts.
314. See nn. 103 and 168.

315. Cf. Is. lv, 7; Neh. ix, 17; 1QH, XXXIX, 2; XLI, 30. For the use of רוכ here, cf. its parallel המון, of line 195.

316. Parts of letters damaged. For expression, cf. Is. lxiii, 15.

317. See n. 224.

318. Cf. Ruth iv, 15.

319. The last two lines may or may not have an actual bearing on the life of the hymnologist, for they may be a mere echo of Ps. xxvii, 10. (Cf. Deut. xxxiii, 9). Elsewhere (1QH, XXXIX, 20) he thanks God for not having forsaken the orphan.

320. The *yodh* is not recorded in O.

321. The reference is no doubt to the members of the Sect. The term occurs often in the Scrolls. It is, however, more common in the Hymns.

322. Following the meaning the V¯ רחם has in Aramaic and Syriac (cf. also the Hebrew in Ps. xviii, 2), I have translated freely "loving-mother". Cf. רחם רחמתים (Jud. v, 30) and רחמה (without *mappiq*. So KK) (Jer. xx, 17), which is parallel with אמי. Cf. also רחמת (Moabite Stone, CNSI, p. 1, 17). A nounal force is sometimes applied in the Mishnah to fem. Pi'el participles. (Cf. e.g. Sab. xx, 1 and Aboth v, 15). See following n.

323. The verse התשכח אשה עולה מרחם בן בטנה (Is. xlix, 15) is obviously in full play here. Does a text which had מרחמת instead of מרחם underlie the phrasing of our line? If so, the translation of the Is. passage will read smoothly thus "Can a woman forget her sucking child; a loving-mother, the son of her womb?" C. Brockelmann, *Grundriss der verglei-chenden Grammatik etc.* I, p. 417, suggests the reading of מרחם or מרחמה (*mem* with *shewa*), meaning a woman about to give birth to her first child. See V.T., VII, 2, p. 213.

324. A compression of Num. xi, 12, substituting the V¯ כול (כלכל) for נשא and לכול מעשיכה for את כל העם. It is interesting to note that Targ., wishing no doubt to avoid anthropomorphism, renders שאהו into סוברהי — a rendering which connotes some of the meaning of כלכל. For an example of the avoidance of an anthropomorphic figure in the Scrolls, cf. perhaps, 1QS, III, 16. For מעשה as parallel with עַ, cf. Is. xix, 25.

INDEXES

Number following semi-colon (;) indicates number of note.

A. GENERAL.

B. AUTORS.

C. REFERENCES.

(a) OLD TESTAMENT

Isaiah
iii, 20; 100 — v, 2; 113 - 4; 127 — vi, 10;
63 — vii, 23; 125 — viii, 4; 54 — ix, 5; 51,
288 - 6; 253 - 19; 133 - 19-20; 133 — x, 18;
151 - 33; 11 — xi, 1; 18 — xvii, 3; 155 -
11; 38, 140 — xviii, 2; 69 — xix, 25; 324
— xxi, 1; 21 - 3; 158, 308 — xxii, 17; 133 —
xxiv, 18; 80 — xxviii, 5; 282 — xxviii, 17;
108 — xxix, 15; 178 - 16; 248 — xxx, 26; 287
— xxxii, 13; 124 — xxxiv, 3; 98 — xxxv, 7; 5
— xxxvi, 4; 191 — xxxvii, 23; 175 - 25; 22
— xxxviii, 19; 223 — xxxix, 8; 277 — xl, 13;
254 - 24; 116 — xli, 11a; 270 - 11-12; 269 -
19; 7, 10 — xlii, 13; 199 — xliii, 19; 7 - 20; 7
- 27; 241 — xliv, 3; 4 — xlviii, 12; 29 —
xlix, 1; 298 - 15; 323 — l, 4; 176, 180 —
li, 3; 7 - 5; 245 - 16; 75, 229 - 19; 179 —
liii, 1; 64 - 2; 116 - 4; 214 — lv, 7; 315 —
lvi, 9; 31 — lvii, 15; 180 - 20; 73 - 21; 257
— lviii, 11; 78 — lix, 21; 229 — lx, 1; 285
- 13; 10 - 21; 19 — lxi, 3; 101 - 9; 133 —
lxii, 3; 282 — lxiii, 15; 218, 316 — lxv, 4;
30

Jeremiah
i, 5; 298 - 9; 229 — ii, 21; 43 — iii, 25;
265 — vi, 25; 130 — vii, 19; 188 — viii,
16; 270 — xi, 10; 241 — xii, 3; 307 —
xiii, 18; 282 — xiv, 9; 134 - 17; 145 - 19;
280 — xv, 16; 278 — xvi, 5; 231 - 19; 293
— xvii, 6; 120, 121 - 8; 25, 117 — xx, 3;
130 - 9; 147, 173 - 10; 130 - 13; 258 - 17;
322 — xxiii, 9; 134 — xxx, 13; 280 —
xxxi, 3; 238 — xxxiii, 6; 277, 280 — xxxvii,
12; 178 - 15; 285 — xxxviii, 11; 173 - 12;
173 — xlii, 6; 266 — xlvi, 5; 130 — xlvii,
2; 71 - 6; 174 — xlviii, 6; 120 — xlix, 3; 38
— l, 29; 217 - 34; 273 — li, 36; 273 - 42;
148

Ezekiel
ii, 7; 266 — v, 13; 200 — vii, 3; 224 - 17;
164 — x, 2; 243 - 15; 35 — xiii, 13; 200 —
xiv, 14; 258 — xv, 12; 282 — xvii, 6; 104
- 22-23; 30 - 24; 17 — xviii, 31; 224 — xix,
13; 5 — xxi, 2; 250 — xxi, 3; 92 — xxviii,
15; 272 - 24; 179 — xxx, 18; 155 — xxxi,
3; 93 - 6; 34 - 13; 34 - 14; 15 — xxxii, 23;
2 — xlvii, 7; 126 - 12; 126, 128

Hosea
ii, 7; 300

Joel
ii, 6; 100 - 20; 96

Amos
iv, 10; 96

Jonah
iii, 4; 53

Micah
ii, 4; 54 — vi, 10; 179

Nahum
ii, 11; 158 — iii, 10; 170 - 17; 48

Habakkuk
ii, 1; 221

Zephaniah
i, 15; 212

Zechariah
ii, 17; 250 — xiii, 1; 80, 102 — xiv, 12; 173
- 20; 93

Malachi
iii, 10; 80, 173

Psalms
i, 3; 128 — ii, 12; 270 — iv, 2; 290 — vi, 6;
203 — viii, 3; 235 — ix, 2; 215 — ix, 6;
230 - 11; 233 - 16; 161 — xii, 5; 171 - 15;
157 — xiii, 6; 243 — xvii, 3; 307 - 13; 312
— xviii, 2; 322 — xxii, 10; 298 - 16; 173
— xxiii, 4; 259 — xxvi, 7; 178 — xxvii,
10; 319 - 13; 64 — xxxi, 8; 223, 290 - 14;
130 — xxxii, 7; 295 — xxxv, 26; 265 —
xxxviii, 12; 209, 211 — xxxix, 10; 182 -
12; 206 — xlii, 6; 154 - 7; 154 - 12; 154 —
xliii, 5; 154 - 8; 227 — xlv, 3; 229 — li, 11;
304 - 15; 304 — lv, 2; 215 — lviii, 2; 293
— lix, 8; 87 — lxiii, 2; 5 — lxvi, 20; 261
— lxviii, 31, 230 — lxix, 12; 220 - 14; 267
- 27; 215 — lxxi, 5-6; 298 - 17; 215 —
lxxiii, 16; 3 — lxxvii, 7; 142 — lxxviii, 23;
80 — lxxix, 8; 241 — lxxx, 16, 110 —
lxxxv, 12; 43 — lxxxvi, 13; 258 — lxxxviii.

4; 143 - 6; 142 — xc, 2; 23 — xci, 5; 153
— xciv, 11; 237 - 19; 218 — xcix, 42; 219
— civ, 20; 31 — cvi, 7; 272 — cvii, 25;
234 — cxviii, 5; 290 — cxix, 16; 240 - 42;
219 - 45; 240 - 50; 238 - 74; 227 - 81; 227
- 123; 208 — cxxxi, 2; 299 — cxxxii, 3; 202
— cxliii, 2; 247 - 3; 230 - 4; 141, 144 - 10;
305 — cxlix, 8; 163, 183 - 9; 183

Proverbs
i, 4; 237 - 6; 190 — iii, 18; 11 - 21; 237 —
v, 15; 3 — viii, 31; 302 — x, 12; 229 - 25;
29 — xii, 8; 308 — xxii, 11; 229 - 27; 230
— xxvii, 5; 44 - 11; 219 — xxix, 4; 234 —
xxx, 6; 275

Job
i, 10; 50 — vii, 13; 203 — viii, 12; 296 -
16-17; 115 — xiv, 9; 22 — xv, 14; 247 —
xxiv, 4; 14 — xxv, 4; 247 — xxvii, 4; 173
— xxix, 19; 27 — xxx, 3; 212 - 12; 165 —
xxxi, 9; 187 - 12; 149 - 22; 159 — xxxiii,
18; 230 - 20; 230 - 22; 230 — xxxvi, 8; 163
— xxxviii, 27; 212 — xxxix, 11; 245 —
xlii, 7; 304 - 8; 304

Canticles
i, 17; 29 — iii, 4; 300 — iv, 12; 13 - 15; 6
— xvii, 13; 261

Ruth
iii, 14; 133 — iv, 15; 318

Lamentations
i, 16; 186, 207, 268 — ii, 11; 207 - 13; 148
— iii, 15; 189 - 49; 207 - 58; 273 — iv, 4;
173 - 14; 45

Ecclesiastes
iv, 8; 253 — viii, 16; 196 — x, 18; 29 —
xii, 9; 190

Esther
i, 10; 263

Daniel
iv, 8-9; 34 — viii, 23-24; 151 — ix, 7; 266
- 8; 266 - 13; 284 - 22; 284 · 24; 151 —
xi, 7; 110 — xii, 4; 48 - 9; 48

Ezra
ix, 9; 216

Nehemiah
ix, 17; 315 — xii, 24; 309

II *Chronicles*
i, 4; 263 — vi, 29; 213 — xii, 3; 295 - 12;
154 — xxvi, 5; 17 — xxxv, 12; 193

(b) APOCRYPHA (R. H. Charles, except for Ben Sira, M. Z. Segal, 1953)

Ben Sira
xiii, 3; 308 — xlv, 8; 282 — li, 6; 230

Jubilees
xxiii, 13; 214

I *Enoch*
xxxii, 3; 15 — lxv, 6; 51 — lxxii, 3-lxxiii,
4; 108 — lxxxiv, 6; 20

II *Enoch*
viii, 3; 11 — xxx, i; 53 — xliii, 2; 250

III *Baruch*
vi, l-viii, 7; 108

Testament of Benjamin
iv, 1; 282

Testament of Judah
iii, 10; 51

Psalms of Solomon
xiv, 2; 11

(c) DEAD SEA SCROLLS

1QH
XXXV, 22; 308 - 35; 191 — XXXVI, 9;
191 - 10; 30 - 11-13; 73 - 17-18; 80 - 18;
167 - 23; 167 - 33; 167, 281 — XXXVII,
8; 159 - 9; 159 - 10; 159 - 12; 159 - 18; 159
- 21; 308 - 21-22; 61- 28; 295 - 29-30; 92 -

30; 103 ⁓ 31; 149 ⁓ 35-36; 51 — XXXVIII,
6, 285 ⁓ 10-14; 264 ⁓ 21; 237 ⁓ 22; 281 ⁓
23; 266, 285 ⁓ 24; 76 ⁓ 26; 263 ⁓ 33-34; 157
⁓ 35; 257 ⁓ 36; 234 — XXXIX, 2; 315 ⁓
9; 76 ⁓ 11; 44, 49 ⁓ 14; 49 ⁓ 16; 153 ⁓ 20;
319 ⁓ 21; 69 ⁓ 23; 270 ⁓ 26; 44 ⁓ 27; 138,
153 ⁓ 32; 49, 138⁓ 33; 30 ⁓ 34; 138 ⁓ 35; 130
⁓ 37; 163 — XL, 15; 20, 68 ⁓ 15-17; 34 ⁓
20; 49 ⁓ 25; 295 ⁓ 26; 107 ⁓ 27; 159 ⁓ 32;
154 — XLI, 2; 159 ⁓ 3; 141 ⁓ 4; 154 ⁓ 10;
180 ⁓ 19 ; 9 ⁓ 21-22 ; 302 ⁓ 22-23 ; 269
⁓ 26; 284 ⁓ 30; 315 — XLV, 4; 284 ⁓ 12;
308 — XLVI, 11-13; 284 ⁓ 22-23; 250 ⁓
23; 103 ⁓ 33; 284 ⁓ 34; 45 — XLVII, 10;
141 ⁓ 15; 308 — XLVIII, 13; 250 ⁓ 18-20;
250 — XLIX, 16; 290 — LI, 8; 133 ⁓ 18;
241 ⁓ 19; 308 — LII, 8; 252 ⁓ 10; 102 ⁓ 12;
102 ⁓ 20; 141 — LIII, (frag. 2) 5; 310 ⁓ 15;
304 — LIV, (frag. 4) 5; 310 — LV, (frag.
2) 6; 295 ⁓ frag. 5; 250 — LVI, frag. 10;
250 ⁓ 11; 250 ⁓ 12; 308 ⁓ 15; 192

1QW

XVI, 1; 21 ⁓ 6; 21 — XVII, 2-4; 309 ⁓ 9;
208 — XIX, 2; 159 — XX, 6; 86 ⁓ 9; 86 ⁓
14; 86 — XXII, 11; 100 — XXIV, 10; 21
— XXVI, 5; 133 — XXVII, 16; 21 —
XXIX, 6; 234 ⁓ 7; 30 — XXXII, 9; 112 —
XXXIII, 5; 108

1QS

III, 15; 277 ⁓ 16; 324 — IV, 7; 282 ⁓ 15-17;
103 — V, 21-24; 250 ⁓ 24; 308 — VI, ;
250 ⁓ 15; 190 — VII, 8; 224 ⁓ 13; 32 —

VIII, 5; 20 — IX, 2; 133 ⁓ 14; 133 — X,
11; 308 ⁓ 14; 262 — XI, 1; 114, 270 ⁓ 3;
102 ⁓ 5; 102 ⁓ 8; 20 ⁓ 22; 32, 248

1Q

P. 67; 133 ⁓ 78, 1.6; 6 ⁓ 103, 6; 108 ⁓ 106
(frag. 4); 155 ⁓ 110, col. I, 17-19; 250 ⁓ 19;
32 ⁓ II, 14-16; 250 ⁓ 21; 250 ⁓ 120, 3-4; 80,
82 ⁓ 123, 23; 302 ⁓ 124, 25; 282 ⁓ 125, last
line; 282 ⁓ 136, 24, 1; 277 ⁓ 137, first Heb.
word; 155 ⁓ 2; 59 ⁓ 140, first Heb. line; 310
⁓ 154, 1, 7; 6

1OIa

V, 17; 133 — XI, 18; 114 — XII, 20; 32
— XIV, 26; 69 — XV, 2; 69 — XVI, 21;
32 ⁓ 22; 32 — XXII, 19; 100 — XXIII,
15; 123 — XXVIII, 4; 32 — XXXI, 3; 29
⁓ 8; 100 — XXXIII, 10; 123 ⁓ 11; 100 —
XXXIV, 23-24; 10 — XXXV, 13; 123 —
XXXVIII, 15; 123 — XXXIX, 4; 32 —
XL, 1; 32 — XLIII, 9; 179 — XLV, 4; 32
⁓ 5; 32 — XLVI, 23; 31 — XLVIII, 29;
123 — XLIX, 2; 123 ⁓ 15-16; 10 — LII, 1;
220 — LIII, 28; 32 — LIV, 3; 123 —
LVII, 16; 178

1QIb

IV, 17; 10 — XIII, 19; 10

1QPHab.

LVIII, col. vii, 2; 151 ⁓ 7; 151 ⁓ 12; 151
— LIX, col. ix, 11; 138 — LX, col. XII, 5;
200

(d) NEW TESTAMENT

S. John
iv, 14; 78

Romans
v, 3; 283

I S. *Peter*
v, 4; 282

(e) TARGUMIN

Targ. (Yer.) on Genesis iii, 24; 53
Targ. Genesis xxvi, 19; 27
Targ. Leviticus xiv, 5; 27 ⁓ 6; 27 ⁓ 50; 27
Targ. Numbers xi, 12; 324
Targ. Judges i, 15; 80

Targ. Jeremiah ii, 13; 27
Targ. Zechariah xiv, 8; 27
Targ. Job xxix, 19; 27
Targ. Canticles iv, 12; 13

(f) RABBINIC SOURCES

Mishnah — Shabbath xx, i; 322
Aboth iv, 13; 282 - v, 8; 308 - 15; 322
Tosefta Kil'ayim III, 3; 19

Talmud — Shabbath 32b; 173 - 33a; 133
Pesaḥim 50a; 93
Baba Qama 92b; 29
Sanhedrin 37a; 32 - 38b; 192
Talmud (Yer.) — 'Erubin 21a; 129
Soṭah 21b; 29

Midrashim
Mid. Rab. on Genesis iii, 24; 53
Mid. Rab. on Leviticus xxxv; 257
Numbers Rab. Sec. 13 end; 133
Mid. Rab. on Canticles ii, 3; 19
Mid. Rab. (Albeck) P. 138; 129
Pesiqta Rab. Sec. 35; 133
Siphri Wa'ethḥannan 21; 173
Tan. (Buber) Gen. v, 38; 29
Wayyosh'a (Yelinek) i, 46; 94